I0011373

Table of Contents

iLife '11 Section

Introduction

Hello. My name is Glen Durdik. I have been using the Macintosh since we bought the Mac SE 1986. Love at first click. I use Macs and PCs on a daily basis for my job. Many people ask me – "Why do you prefer the Mac?" Well, nowadays the decision is a lot more complicated as the two main operating systems blur features and look and act the same. But there is a difference that probably will never change (it was once true)… Apple makes their hardware and the OS to run in it. One company devoted to offering the best possible hardware and an OS that is tested to work perfectly on this hardware. For the PC users, this means having to find different drivers for all of the hardware on your computer. On a Mac…it just works. OK. I admit that is 99% true.

Why this guide? Well, for those "switchers" out there, this is a good intro the Mac OS. For the newbies and more experienced users, I hope that you will learn a thing or two about the Mac experience and more importantly – L♥VE your Mac more then ever. This is the first section of the **Essence of the Macintosh Experience** book. It includes a short guide to buying a new Macintosh, goes over the desktop, all the menus in the OS, System Preferences, Airport Utility, Disk Utility, MobileMe, Mail.app, a few other cool Apple applications, a few other Utilities, important Apple websites, Safari 4.0 and last – a short guide to keeping your Mac healthy and happy. I also cover the new install process of 10.6 and highlight its new features. A 169 page guide to what makes the Macintosh a Macintosh – a special device that we all cherish daily. The other two guides available cover iLife '09 and iWork '09. In these manuals – I explain all the different elements that make up the workspace and the menus for each application.

- Glen Durdik

Buying Tips – Finding the best Mac to meet your needs

Unlike non-Apple branded PCs – that have a zillion choices to choose from – in a Mac world – there are very few. This makes your decision easier – Yes, but there are few items to keep track of before buying the best computer in the known universe.

First, let's start with the three basic questions a potential buyer must ask.

What am I going to use this awesome new Mac for ?,

Do I want a laptop or desktop? and

How much money can I spend on this new powerful and fun to use Mac?

OK. You made the right decision – Mac OS and Apple hardware is the right choice for you. Next, make a list of what you want to use it for. This could be casual web surfing to full-blown video editing. Luckily, Apple (sort of) has a Mac for every type of user. Basically, Apple has a "Consumer" line of products and a "Pro" line of products. This applies to their laptop and desktop units. Let me sum up the consumer line first.

> **Mac Mini** – A great small – yet powerful Mac that does not include a monitor. This is the least expensive Mac desktop. It is good for the majority of uses of a typical Mac user. That is email access, web browsing, storing music (iTunes) and some sort of productivity suite for word processing and spreadsheets (iWork is Apple's version – which I discuss in the iWork section of this series). Some users use this in a "no monitor required" scenario. This could be a file server, web server or media center - as opposed to an Apple TV for example. (New model available as Server – has two HDs and not optical drive)So… small and good performer – the Mac Mini.

iMac – This is Apple's "all-in-one" unit. The unit as a whole runs faster then the Mac Mini. This is Apple's idea of the perfect consumer PC. Unlike the Mac Mini – the hardware inside has a few more options to chose from. It has what most buyers want and is a breeze to setup as the monitor is built-in. More choices, faster, setup in no time – the iMac. (Now has a 21 or 27 inch LED monitor and SD Card Slot)

MacBook - This is Apple's consumer laptop. Great features and screen (13"). Unless you need a bigger screen, this unit is perfect for most day to day tasks done on a Mac.

MacBook Air – Not the fastest laptop – but really, really thin. If you want a laptop that has a normal sized screen that weights a lot less – this is for you. It is premium priced because of its slender design.

Not excited yet? How about a Pro model...

Mac Pro – Man...these suckers are fast. These have the most configurable options of all the desktops. Fastest memory, hard drives and processors. Way cool. Way expensive.

MacBook Pro – Fastest laptops offered by Apple. Offers two larger screen sizes. Great for the business traveler. (13", 15" or 17" screens available.) Now includes an SD Memory card slot.

OK. You now know what Apple offers. You now have an idea of what you want to purchase. SHOW ME THE MONEY...for options of course.

Options to be aware of...

Hard Drive – There are two things to watch for. **Speed – in RPMs**. The higher the number – the better. Laptops usually are 5400 – while desktops are 7200. The Macbook Air also offers a SSD hard drive - which has no moving parts. For general Mac Nirvana – the hard drives Apple offers are fine for what they are used for. Of course, if you purchase a Mac Pro for video work the need for extremely fast drives does exist. So, be aware of the number – but it is not a deal breaker. **Size - GBs.** The larger the number – the more data you can store on it.

Memory – Macs LOVE Memory. You will grow to LOVE your Mac. Be kind to your Mac and purchase enough memory you can afford. This will make your experience on the Mac a lot smoother. I am not saying that the default memory on say a Mac Mini is going to be horrible – but – things will just seem smoother and quicker with more. Again, buy as much memory as you can. **Note:** Apple charges an arm and leg for memory. Depending on what model you chose – it would be cheaper to buy third party memory (always buy from vendor that gives it a lifetime warranty) and easy to install. Some might require a tech to install – like the Mini – therefore for convenience – it might be easier to buy Apple memory and have them install it.

Processor – The larger the number – the faster the Mac. Consumer Macs are fine for most applications. If you require a Mac that is going to have very processor intensive applications running – then go with the Mac Pro. (Available in some models as dual-core or quad core)

Video Card – In the iMac and Mac Pro – Apple offers choices. Generally, the more expensive the card – the more memory it has on board and is faster then a less expensive card. My take... if you can – purchase the highest card. You might turn into a serious gamer or video producer and the faster card will be worth it. If not – no worries – it should be fine.

Screen size – Mini does not come with a monitor. There are two choices for the iMac. The sky is the limit with the Mac Pro. The MacBook is the smallest laptop. The MacBook Pro has two larger screen sizes. In regard to the iMac... I prefer the larger screen. Why? It makes using everyday applications a lot easier to see and if you use a lot of apps at once – more room to spread them out. It is big though – so measure where it would go and see if it fits!!

So, that is a breakdown of the models Apple offers and the key options all Macs have. My suggestions –

Have a monitor and keyboard. Basic Internet User. Love using iLife – don't need it to be blazing fast – Mac Mini or MacBook.

Need a Mac that can do the majority of tasks without bogging down – iMac.

You just won the lottery and find yourself in hunt for a Mac – the Mac Pro or MacBook Pro. Well, if you are in a business that needs that speed and expansion capability then get a Mac Pro also.

Last, if you are still in the preliminary stages of a purchase – go to http://buyersguide.macrumors.com/. This a good guide that mentions all Macs and iPods and gives you a heads-up when the new version of the model you like is might be due for an upgrade. Not an exact science, but it might be a good idea to wait a month if it suggests a new model is imminent.

A note on AppleCare. I always recommend purchasing this extended warranty. Apple is great for service and repairs. However, if something breaks out of warranty – Apple parts for the most part are very expensive to replace. Play it safe and purchase the AppleCare warranty.

Mouse Basics

(Here a Click…there a click…everywhere a double-click click)

Using a mouse has become second nature to most computer users around the globe. Before I begin with any other topics, I feel I should shed some light as to how the mouse functions on a Mac.

Unselected Mac Folder/ Document

If you click on the item… it becomes highlighted.

If you double-click on the item it will either open the folder or open the file in the program the created it.

If you click on the item and press the return key, you can rename the item.

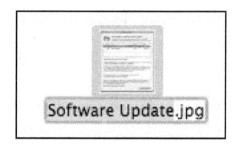

If you "right-click" on the item, you get a contextual menu. Most mice have two buttons. The button on the right is the one you use to right-click. You can also hold down the control button while clicking to perform the same task.

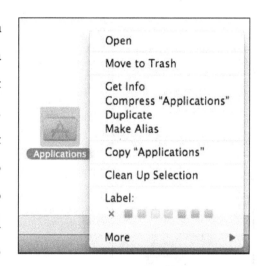

Moving Files around

If you are navigating between folders on your hard drive and move one item to another folder – the item is moved from the original folder to the new folder. If you hold down the option key while doing this, the item is copied and now there are two copies on your hard drive. If you hold down the command and option keys while moving the item – you create an alias of the item. An alias is just a small file that links back to the original item on your hard drive(s).

The Finder

The Finder is the heart of what makes a Mac a Mac. It is actually a program that is constantly running. It is the icon all the way to the left of your dock. What is a dock? Not sure, then you are reading the right guide.

First, I would like to start with a screenshot of the desktop. A desktop includes all the items you see when you are finished booting up your Mac or logging into it. It is shown on the next page.

The Main items are the **Menu Bar**, the **Dock**, and icons showing what **Devices are Available**. In this case, I have my internal hard drive named Macintosh HD, two external drives, a flash drive and CD. When you insert a CD or DVD to attach storage device it will show up below your Macintosh HD icon (or below the item closest to the HD).

I would like to start by going over the Dock. The Dock is a means of having quick access to commonly used applications or documents. In 10.5, there are two folders added to the Dock by default. These are the Documents folder and the Downloads Folder. You can add more folders to the Dock if you wish. I will continue this discussion on the page following the screenshot of the Mac Desktop.

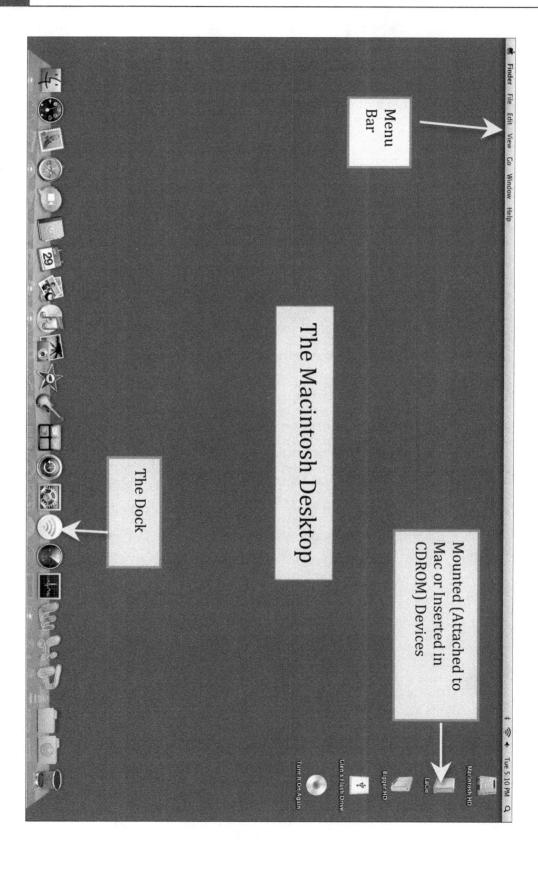

Menu Bar

The Macintosh Desktop

The Dock

Mounted (Attached to Mac or Inserted in CDROM) Devices

Dock in Depth

Above is an example of a typical dock. In this instance, it is on the bottom of the screen. It can also be on the left or the right of the screen. Here are a few key points for the dock…

If you move your mouse directly over the icon of the application, it displays the name of the file or application.

On the left is an example of Applications in the Dock. Please notice that two of them have a bluish-white dot below the icon. This means the application is open or running in the background.

If you move your mouse over the application you chose and press and the mouse button, you are given what is called a "contextual" menu. This means that the menus shown depends on what you are clicking on. This is also available when you right-click on an application, folder or document elsewhere on your hard drive or removable media.

The series of increasingly smaller lines divides the application section of the dock and the document/folder and Trash.

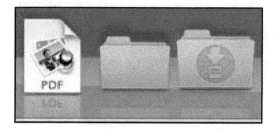

Here is an example of the items you can put on the other side of the divider. Next to the PDF file is the **Document folder** for your account as well as the **Downloads folder**. (This is the icon with the arrow in it)

If you put a folder on the right side of the divider and click on the folder, the folder springs to the right to show all documents or other items in the folder. If you have a lot of items, the Mac will show it as a plain list – not arching to the right.

The item all the way to the right on you dock is the Trashcan (**Silver Waste Basket icon**). Drag any unwanted items to the trashcan to delete. You **MUST** select Empty Trash from the File Menu to remove the item. The Trashcan is also one way to eject removable media. This is shown to the right of the trashcan icon on the right. Notice that the Trash Icon changes to an arrow with a line on it. This means the Mac will remove the item you want when it reaches the trash can.

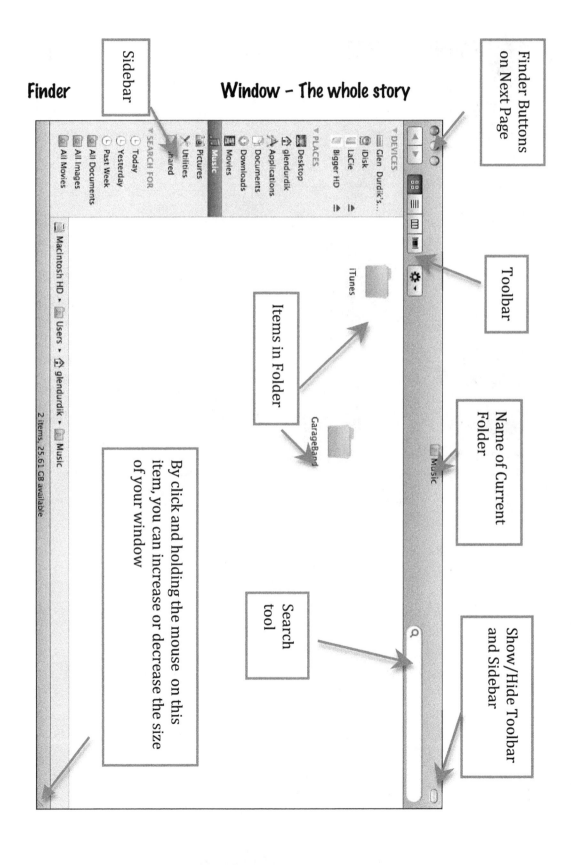

This button will give you the option to close the current file you are working on or close the folder you are currently in.

This button will "minimize" your current item to the Dock. You can then go to the dock and reopen the item later. (Document is still in use.)

This item will expand or decrease the size of the window you have open.

If you want to go to the previous folder or forward from a later folder, click on the left button to go back and the right button to go forward.

These four items are the choices for your "view." I will go show examples of each later on.

 This is the action button. Depending on what you are doing, you are given various options to choose from. Below are the options in a typical finder window.

> New Folder
> New Burn Folder
> Open
>
> Get Info
>
> Clean Up
> Arrange By   ▶
> Show View Options

Very Important Function in OS X - Save As... Option Window

Why am I bringing up the Save option here? Well, I have received a lot calls about not being able to save to the place the user wants. I want to share the basics here so that you have no trouble saving where you like and how you want to save. I am using Office 2008 in the following examples.

To the left is the default Save or Save as window. Notice that you can name the file on the

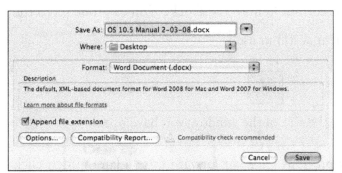

very top and save to the desktop. If you click on Desktop, you are given a list of standard locations and recent folders. Not many options right? Well, see the little blue arrow next to file name? Here is the trick. Click on that arrow. This then brings up the following (more complete) save option. You now can navigate to exactly the folder you like by clicking on the sidebar and choosing the drive or

device you want to save. All the way on the bottom left is the option to create a new folder. This is useful for organizing your documents and not saving all of them to the desktop. Click on **Save** to save your work.

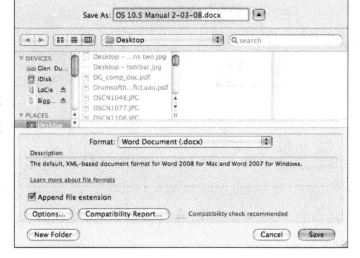

Please note the Format: option. This is some form is usually available in every application. Below are the options available for Word 2008. This option is key if you need to make your document accessible to users who don't have the same version of the software as you or if you want to change the type of graphic in iPhoto. (.Jpg to other format)

✓ Word Document (.docx)

Common Formats
Word 97-2004 Document (.doc)
Word Template (.dotx)
Word 97-2004 Template (.dot)
Rich Text Format (.rtf)
Plain Text (.txt)
Web Page (.htm)
PDF

Specialty Formats
Word Macro-Enabled Document (.docm)
Word Macro-Enabled Template (.dotm)
Word XML Document (.xml)
Word 2003 XML Document (.xml)
Single File Web Page (.mht)
Word Document Stationery (.doc)
Speller Custom Dictionary (.dic)
Speller Exclude Dictionary (.dic)
Word 4.0-6.0/95 Compatible (.rtf)

Mac OS X Menus

The Mac OS has always had Menus available on the top of your screen. I will go in detail of all the Menus and their submenus or the Finder. Each Application has their own Menus, but their layout is consistent between applications. File Menu and Edit Menu will be in the same location for example. To access a Menu, move your mouse over the menu you want and then click the mouse button. All of the available options are then shown in a drop down box. If you see a black triangle all the way to the right of the menu option, this means there is a submenu for that option.

Apple Menu

To the left is the complete window of the Apple Menu. I will go over each in detail on the following pages.

About this Mac:

This window gives you general info on your wondrous device known as a Mac. Notice it has OS version installed, processor type and memory. Software update is discussed below. If you click on **More Info…**, you launch System profiler. This utility gives you much greater detail on the best purchase you ever made. System profiler is discussed in the Utilities Section of this manual.

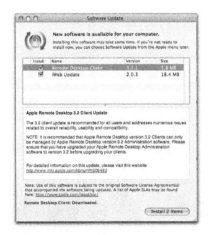

Software Update:

Your Mac is setup to automatically check for software updates. In the case shown on the left, there are two updates to be installed. Click on Install… to update your Mac. You must then type in the administrator password to complete the process. **Note: It is wise to wait a few days before upgrading. By then, others will have found out if it works great or has bugs.**

System Preferences:

There are 26 standard preferences to modify. I have four additional installed. Notice that they are grouped into four different groups. It may sound like a lot to learn, but with the help of this written manual and few trips to it, I am sure it

will become second nature to you. I have a whole section devoted to these preferences later on.

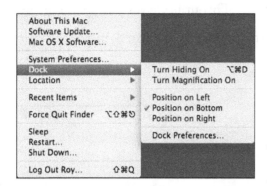

Dock Preferences:

First, here is an example of a submenu. When you move your mouse to the word Dock, the screen to the left is shown. Here is where you can decide where you want the dock to be shown, have it hidden until used or turn on magnification. Magnification makes the icon you move over expand and grow bigger. This is useful if you have a ton of items on your dock as the icons adjust and get smaller as you add more.

Location:

If you have a laptop, this is a great way to have different network settings for every location you travel to. Network Preferences is the option you chose if you want to edit your locations.

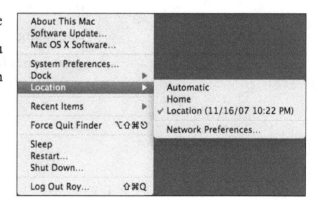

Recent Items:

This option shows your most recently used applications, documents and if you use it – your servers. You can also clear all items via the last option on this menu. The number of items shown can be adjusted in the Appearance option of the System Preferences.

Force Quit…:

Yes, Macs do lock up. The first thing to stop the dreaded "beach ball of death" is to try force quitting the application that is stuck. On the right, you see a list of many applications. Choose the one that is giving you grief and click on the Force Quit button on the bottom right of the menu. You can also do this via the dock or pressing the (command) ⌘ + OPTION and ESC Keys.

Sleep:

This puts your tired Mac to sleep. Depending on your settings, your monitor and if you choose – your hard drive will go to sleep mode. Press any key to wake the sleeping Mac up. I recommend a good 8-hour sleep every night for proper Mac functioning during the day.

Restart:

If you want to restart your Mac, this is where you would do it. Notice that there is a timer that will automatically restart if you do nothing after choosing this option.

Shutdown:

Had enough fun using the world's best computer for now? Here is where you turn off your Mac.   NEVER unplug your Mac while it is on. Always use this command whenever possible.

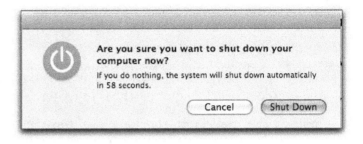

Log Out (name)...

If you have more than one user account on your Mac, you use this option to close your account and bring you to the Login Window.

Finder Menu

Complete Finder Menu:

To the left is the full Finder Menu. I will go into further detail of each option below.

Finder Preferences:

Here you are given four main categories of options. The first is **General** – which is shown to the right. By the default, all hard drives, external disks and other external media are shown on the desktop. You can also chose what location opens when you choose New Finder window. By default it is Home, but it could by any other folder you chose. If you have **Always open Folders in new window**, then a new window will open with its contents. If not chosen, the previous window will not be shown on the screen. **Spring-loaded folders'** delay can be adjusted in this option as well.

Labels:

Here you can change the name of each label. Labels (colors) are put onto a file or folder by clicking on an item and selecting Get Info on the item. You can then give that item whatever color you want at bottom of the Get Info window.

Sidebar:

When you open a new Finder window, the items you display on the left side of the window are chosen by what you pick in this option. Notice that I unchecked **All Images** and **All Movies**. You can also add any folder you like by just dragging into the Sidebar. For example, if you want easy access to Microsoft Office programs or files, then you can add them here. This is not done in the Sidebar shown to the right – it is done on the Sidebar of an open Finder window.

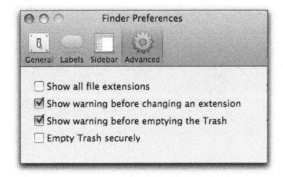

Advanced:

Show all file extensions: Most application's extension is shown. If you chose this option, the biggest change is adding .app to all applications. (Firefox.app for the web browser) You should leave the next two options alone. If you choose, Empty Trash securely all items deleted are GONE. There are utilities available that can retrieve files deleted the normal "non-secure" way.

Hide Finder:

This option hides all other items except for the application you are working on.

Hide Others:

This hides all items except the Finder.

Show All:

This restores all windows – shows Finder and Applications.

File Menu

New Finder Window	⌘N
New Folder	⇧⌘N
New Smart Folder	⌥⌘N
New Burn Folder	
Open	⌘O
Open With	▶
Print	
Close Window	⌘W
Get Info	⌘I
Compress	
Duplicate	⌘D
Make Alias	⌘L
Quick Look "Macintosh HD"	⌘Y
Show Original	⌘R
Add to Favorites	⇧⌘T
Move to Trash	⌘⌫
Eject "Macintosh HD"	⌘E
Burn "Macintosh HD" to Disc...	
Find by Name...	⇧⌘F
Label:	
✕ ▪ ▪ ▪ ▪ ▪ ▪	

Complete File Menu:

While working in the Finder...

New Finder Window: Creates a new window with the contents of the folder you just opened.

New Folder: Creates an "Untitled" folder in the window that is currently open. You can rename it while creating it or click on a folder and hit the return key.

New Smart Folder: Allows you to create folders based upon a search. I did a search for "**.doc**" files and all of those files showed up. Next, I clicked on "Save." This is shown here -

I can then name the folder and where I want it stored.

New Burn Folder: This creates a folder that is used to store items you would like to "burn" to a CD or DVD later on.

Open: Opens your document or application. You can double-click on a document or application as well. **Note: Dock items are just one-click - not two.**

Get Info:

There are seven submenus in the **Get Info** window.

Spotlight: This is an Apple technology for providing fast searches.

General: Here you can see what type of document it is, where it is located, when it was created and modified, see what color label it has, make it into a Stationary Pad or lock the file.

More Info: Gives you additional info on the file.

Name and Extension: This gives you the name and what file extension it has. You can rename the file here.

Open With: In the example to the right, the document is a picture (.jpg) file. Notice that it defaults to Preview. You can change that setting to any program that supports viewing **.jpg** files.

Preview: This give a small preview of the file.

Sharing and Permissions: All documents and files have permissions assigned to them. I am currently logged on as top user shown on the right and have Read and Write privileges. This means I can modify the document. The other two accounts can only Read the file.

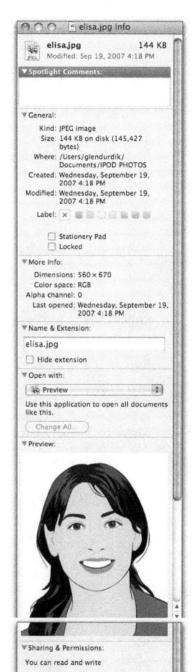

Back to the options after Get Info...

Compress: Converts any item you choose to a .zip file. The file you created is smaller in file size. This is useful when sending large files via emails.

Duplicate: Makes an exact copy of what you choose to duplicate.

Make Alias: If you use a certain program and file on a daily basis, you might want to put an alias of that item on your desktop. Just double-click on the alias you created and the file will be opened.

Quick look "File or other item:" This gives you a small preview of the item you have selected.

Show Original: If you click an alias, this will bring up the exact location of the original file.

Add to Favorites/Sidebar: Adds the item to your favorites or the Sidebar of the Finder Window.

Move to Trash: Instead of dragging the item or external drive to the trash can manually, you can use this menu option instead.

Eject "*Name*" If you want to eject a device, you can use this menu option.

Burn "*Name*" **to Disc...:** You can burn the selected folder or device by using this command.

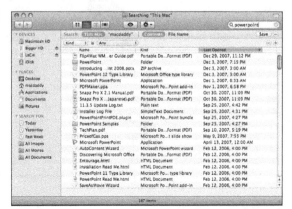

Find:

This option allows you to search any of your attached devices for a file or application.

There are a lot of options to choose from when you search. They include: content or file name, kind, date created, date modified, etc. Kind is the default. Click on Kind to bring up these other options.

Label:

This allows you to organize your data by giving each item a unique color. For example - blue for Work documents.

Edit Menu

Complete Edit menu:

Undo/Can't Undo:

This is where you go if you want to undo the last option you preformed. If you decide you want to keep the change, select "Undo (option you chose).

Cut:

Deletes the selection you have chosen.

Copy:

Makes a copy of what you have selected.

Paste:

Inserts whatever you copied into the area after your mouse is positioned.

Select All:

This selects all items in a folder or all the words in a document. Useful if you want to delete everything in folder or in a document in one quick action.

Show Clipboard:

The clipboard is where the Mac stores copied items. Parts of a document or a picture from the Internet you just copied for example.

Special Characters:

This option shows you all of the special characters that are available with the fonts you have installed. Fonts are the different types of type you can **choose** in your **document**.

View Menu

Complete View Menu:

The four main view options here determine how your open folders look. They are: Icon View, List View, Columns View and Cover Flow View.

Icon View:

This view displays all items as an icon inside the window. Notice that the icon shown is a small preview of the document.

List View:

Here all items in the window are shown as list of files.

Column View:

This is modified list view. In the example on the right, I clicked on iChat icons. Notice how the contents appear in the new column next to folder you are opening. This will repeat until you opened the folder you want.

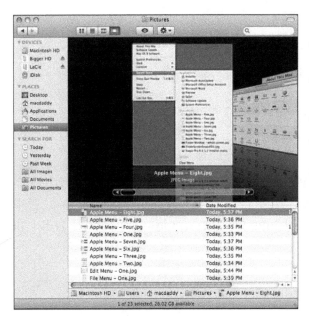

Cover Flow View:

Those who have used iTunes before will recognize this view. It is particularly useful when searching for a certain picture in a folder with a lot of items.

Clean Up Selection:

This will, well, "clean up" your icons while viewed as Icon View.

Arrange By:

If you are in the Icon view, this will arrange your icons by various criteria. The options available are shown on the right.

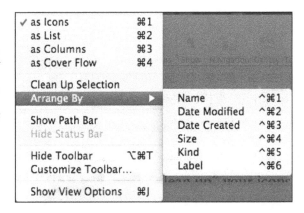

Show/Hide Path Bar:

This option will display the "path" or exact location as to where the item you clicked on is located. Here is an example for my iTunes folder –

Show/ Hide Toolbar:

Here you can enable or disable the toolbar found in your finder window. Below is an example of a default toolbar.

Customize Toolbar...:

This is where you can add or delete items to the toolbar (shown above). The options you can choose from are shown to the left. You can also choose to view the items as text or text and icons.

Show View Options:

You are given many options to customize your "view." The first option allows you to always open folders in an Icon view. The next two options determine Icon size and the Grid spacing. Note: If you choose to "Clean UP" your window, it defaults to square grid. This is where you would modify the grid settings. You can also change Text size or the position of the Label (Bottom or Right.) Next, you can show item info, icon preview or arrange by the following choices...

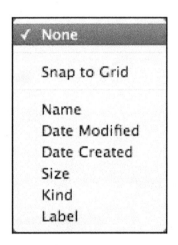

Background:

You can change the color of the finder window from white to any color you choose or a picture as well.

Go Menu

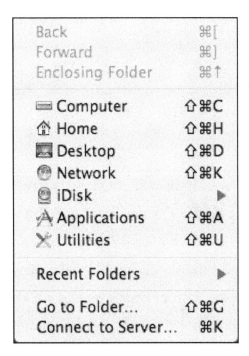

This menu is used to navigate around your Mac. You can choose **Back** or **Forward** (folders) or go to any of the default locations listed on the left (Desktop, Home Folder, etc.) You can also go to recent folders, type in a folder location or connect to a server.

The **Connect to Server**... window is below. If you are on a network, but not sure of the IP address, then you can choose Browse to see all available servers. You can also save the server for future access.

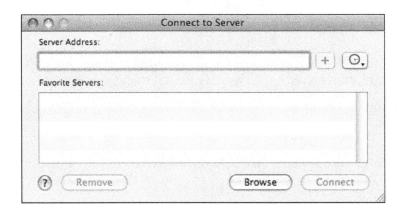

Window Menu

Minimize   ⌘M
Zoom
Cycle Through Windows   ⌘ `

Bring All to Front

✓ Pictures

The first two options in this menu are the same as two of the finder buttons. **Minimize** takes the active window and puts it into the dock. The document is still open and can be again accessed by clicking on the icon for it on the dock. **Zoom** expands or contracts the window. **Cycle Through Windows** goes through all open finder windows open. **Bring All to Front** brings all open windows to the front of your screen. Last, the menu shows you all open finder windows. In the example above, there is only one open folder – Pictures.

Help Menu

Need advice on how to perform a task while working on your Mac? This is a great resource to provide that assistance. The best way to show the menu is provide an example of it in action. Here, I am having a problem printing. I accessed the Help menu and typed

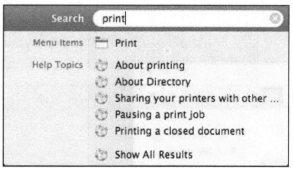

in "print." The screen to the right is what appears. It displays the Menu Item if it exists.

Here is what would happen if I clicked on **Menu Items** -

It went to the File Menu and pointed out exactly where the Print Command is.

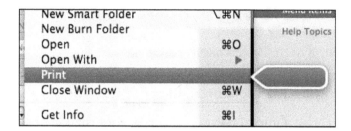

If you choose all results for Print, you get 25 items and the relevance towards your question. This is shown below. Click on the topic heading to go to that help topic.

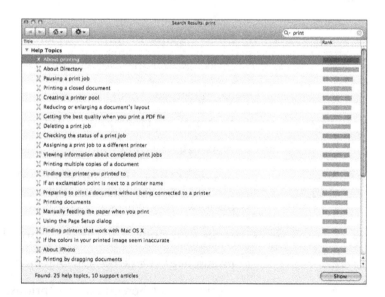

System Preferences

(Dock Icon For System Preferences)

OK. Now you know how what makes up your Mac desktop and have an idea where every menu is and what options are available in each. Time to dig a little deeper into the Heart of Mac OS. The System Preferences pane (window) gives you numerous options for configuring your Mac. Some you may never look at, some just a glance. But, as you will see - some are **KEY** and having knowledge where to look and what to configure will make your days using your Mac – once again have you saying, "Why did I ever use Windows?"

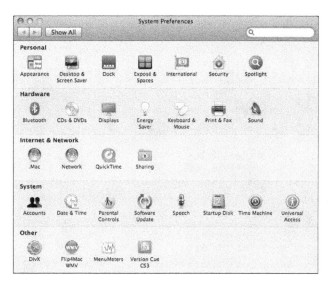

Here again is the complete **System Preferences** pane. Again, note that Apple has grouped them into similar groups: **Personal**, **Hardware**, **Internet & Network**, **System** and if you have any others - **Other**. If you look over all of the options, you will see that most options seem obvious. Dock for Dock preferences, Desktop and Screensaver for Desktop and Screen Saver Options. But there are a lot more and I will go over all in the next few pages. Note: The purple colored question mark at the bottom of each pane. If you click on it, you get help for the pane you currently have open.

System Preferences - Personal

Appearance Pane:

This window is broken down into four sections.

Appearance – gives you the option of changing the font color of highlighted menu option. The default is blue – you can change it to graphite (grey).

Highlight Color - allows you to change the

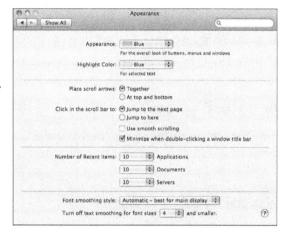

color of the highlighted text. (Select the text that you want to change its characteristics or Cut, Copy or Paste for example). Here you are given more than two color choices.

Place scroll arrows: - determines where the up and down scroll arrows are located. Some prefer them together on the bottom, while others like having to move their mouse all the way to the top of the window to access the up scroll arrow.

Click in the scroll bar to: - allows your set the action when you click on the scroll bar. For example, if you click on the bar above the blue location icon, then you will go back one page.

Use smooth scrolling: - When turned on, your Mac does not make your screen "jump" when you scroll.

Minimize when double-clicking a window title bar – this option will shrink the document down and place it in the dock. The file is still open – just click on the icon in the dock to re-open it.

Number of Recent Items: - Here you can set how many Applications, Documents and Servers will be kept in the Apple Menu. The default is 10 each.

Font smoothing style: - Depending on the screen you use, adjusting this setting will make your fonts appear better on the screen.

Turn off text smoothing for font sizes (number) and smaller – As the font size gets smaller font smoothing may actually make fonts look worse. Here you can set what size to turn it off.

Desktop and Screen Saver Pane:

To the right is the standard **Desktop Pane**. Note that you can change the picture at specified times and if you click on the + sign you can add your own folders.

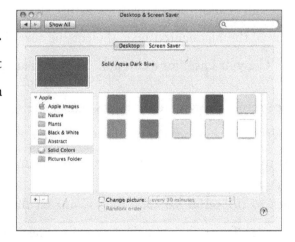

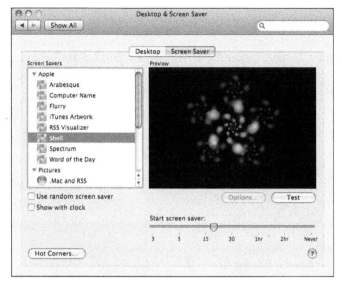

To the left is the standard **Screen Saver Pane.** Note that you can choose a random screen saver, show it with a clock, test the screen saver and determine when you want it to kick in.

Dock Pane:

This pane determines various aspects of the Dock. You can also access some Dock Prefs from Dock option in the Apple Menu. Besides the basic set of options in the Apple Menu - this adds the ability to

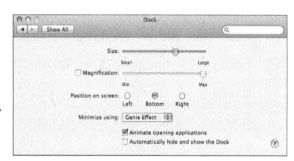

manually set the size, the size of the magnification (if you have it enabled), the effect when you minimize (Genie or Scale), animate the opening of applications and last, option to automatically show or hide the Dock.

Expose and Spaces Pane:

The screen to the right is the Expose Pane. Active Screen corner allows you to assign each corner of your screen a special command such as Sleep. Expose is cool way of seeing the window you want by using one of three keyboard shortcuts. First, **All windows (F9)** shrinks all windows and shows all of them on your screen. The second – **Application windows (F10)** highlights the active application. Last the **Show Desktop (F11)** moves ALL open windows off the screen and shows you just your desktop. Note: These keyboard commands are customizable.

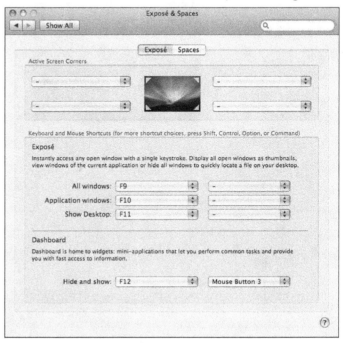

Dashboard: This is a cool feature in OS X. There are a few pre-installed and you can download many, many more. Examples are a clock and calendar – shown here…

The default keyboard key is **F12**.

International Pane:

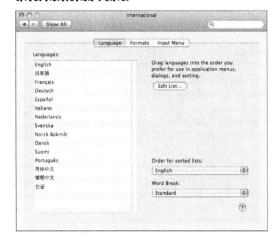

This pane contains three main options. They are Language, Formats and Input Menu. The window to the left shows the first – **Language**. This is where you set your default language for Menus, Dialogs and sorting.

Format:

This is where you customize how dates, times, numbers and currency are shown. You can also change the measurements to metric if you like.

Input Menu:

If you are using special devices to input certain languages, this is where you would activate correct codes for the language in question.

Security Pane:

There are three main options in this pane. Understanding how the Mac provides security for each user account is key. Better safe then find all you files copied or suddenly missing.

The first option is **General**. At the top of the screen is the ability to ask for a password from waking up from sleep or a screen saver. The next section applies to all accounts.

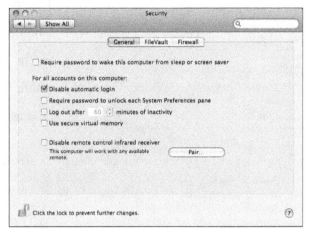

Disable automatic login: If you ENABLE automatic login, there is no password needed to log onto to the computer when it is turned on. If it is disabled, the user account and password is needed to get on. **Require password to unlock each System Preferences Pane:** As you will see having access to any or all of the System Prefs could be very bad. Locking them should give you peace of mind that critical settings are not going to be played with. **Log out after (number) minutes of inactivity:** If you are worried that someone might try to access your account while you are away from your Mac – then this option will log you out at the time interval you select. **Use secure virtual memory:** protects items stored in memory also. **Disable remote control infrared receiver:** Would you want your kid from turning on Front Row from a few feet away? This is where you turn off the infrared.

Note: The yellow lock at the bottom right of the screen. If you click on it, only the people with the admin password can open the preference pane and modify it.

FileVault Option:

FileVault is an option, that when turned on, will encrypt your home folder. You SHOULD set a master password. This will allow you to access any **FileVault** account. Notice that I have it currently turned off. **Note:** If you turn this on...you need additional hard drive space for the files.

Firewall Pane:

Mac OS X has a built-in Firewall. Here is where you access the options. **Allow all incoming connections** is the most open option, while **Set Access for specific services and applications** is the most secure. To add applications,

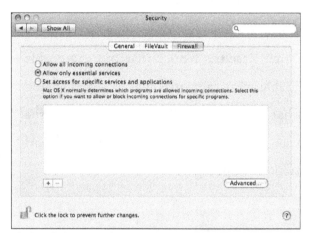

click on the little plus sign on the bottom left of the window. If you chose the second two options, you have access to the **Advanced** tab located at the bottom of this window.

Below is an example of the **Advanced** window.

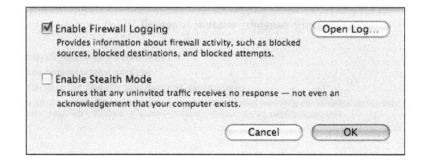

Enable Firewall Logging – Provides info on activity with the Firewall.

Enable Stealth Mode – This turns your Mac into a device that only you can see. Actually, if your Mac receives traffic from an unwanted source, it will not respond. Therefore, your Mac is "invisible" on the Internet. Not to the naked eye – that is Apple's next big idea.

Spotlight Pane:

Spotlight is method of quickly searching your hard drive for a file or folder. The first window is Search Results. Notice that you can enable or disable what categories will be searched and in what order they will be displayed. At the bottom of the screen are the two keyboard shortcuts for Spotlight.

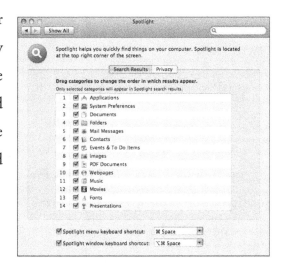

Privacy:

The second window is Privacy. Here you can tell Spotlight what folders NOT to search.

System Preferences - Hardware

Bluetooth Pane:

The first Hardware Pane is Bluetooth. Notice that I do not have any devices paired. You can also turn on or off Bluetooth Power and make you Mac be Discoverable. To add a device, click on the small plus sign at the bottom of the screen. You can also decide if you want

the Bluetooth Status available in the menu bar. All the way on the bottom right of the window is **Advanced....**

This screen is shown here -

There are five major options. The first will open the Bluetooth Setup Assistant at startup if paired devices are not available. The second will wake your Mac if the device is used. (Hitting a key on a Bluetooth keyboard to awake from sleep. The third determines if you want to be alerted if a Bluetooth audio device attempts to connect. The fourth allows you to share your Internet connection.

The last will turn on or off the serial port used by your Mac for Bluetooth communication.

CDs and DVDs Pane:

This is pretty straightforward. Choose what you want you Mac to do when certain types of CDs or DVDs are inserted.

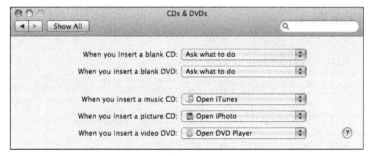

Displays Pane:

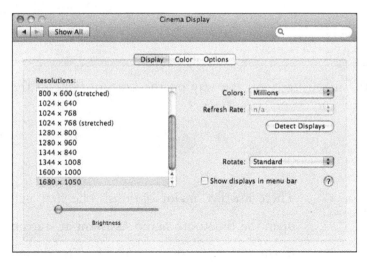

(Shown using an Apple Cinema Display)

Resolutions: Basically, the LARGER the number (1680 x 1050 vs. 800 x 600) the smaller the images are on the screen.

Colors: The higher the number (millions in this case) the more colors will be shown on the screen.

Refresh Rate: Used with older CRT displays.

Detect Displays: Used when you have more than one monitor attached to your Mac.

Rotate: You can rotate your image 90 or 180 degrees for example.

Show displays in menu bar: If you select this option, you will see a small monitor icon in menu bar and several features found here can be accessed.

Brightness: Darkens or Lightens the image on your screen.

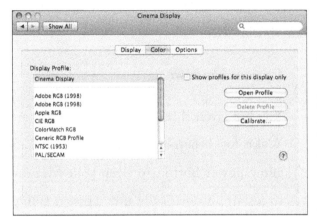

Color:

Each display has a unique profile. Apple has supplied many of them. If you want to calibrate (modify this profile to your tastes) – click on the **Calibrate...** button.

Options:

On the Cinema Display – the power button can either turn the display on or off, put the system to sleep (or wake it) or do nothing. The only other option here is do you want to disable the brightness buttons.

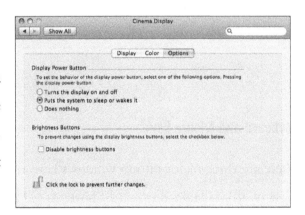

Energy Saver Pane:

There are two major options located in this pane. The first is **Sleep**. The first two options determine the time interval of when you want to put the computer or display to sleep when

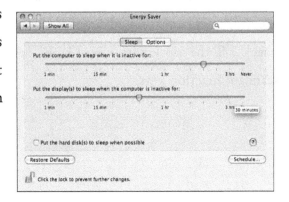

your Mac has been inactive for X amount of minutes. You can also put the your hard drives to sleep by checking the box at the bottom left of the screen.

On the bottom right of the screen is the **Schedule...** option. You can set your Mac to Start up/wake your Mac at a certain time. The second option gives you the ability to put your Mac to sleep. **Restart** or **Shutdown** at a certain time as well.

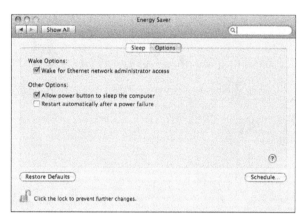

Options window:

You are given three options here. They are: Wake for Ethernet network admin access, allow power button to sleep your Mac and to restart automatically after a power failure.

Keyboard and Mouse Pane:

There are three major option windows here and a list of all available Keyboard Shortcuts. The first – keyboard is shown to the right. Basic settings such as the Key Repeat Rate and Delay Until Repeat are accessed here. You can also check off the option to use F1, F2, etc. as standard function keys.

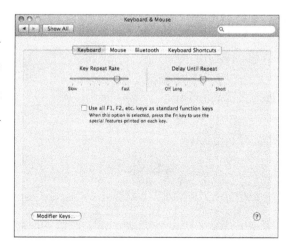

Modifier Keys can be defined by clicking on the button on the bottom left of the screen. Here is what it looks like –

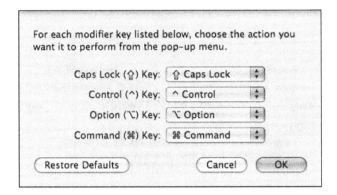

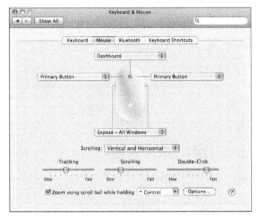

Mouse:

There are numerous settings available for you to configure. Each mouse button can be given a variety of commands.

Bluetooth:

If you have a Bluetooth mouse and/or keyboard, this is where you can find the status of the devices. At the bottom right of the screen, there is the **Set Up New Device...** button that will allow you to pair a new device.

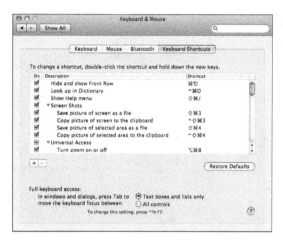

Keyboard Shortcuts:

This is a list of all available keyboard shortcuts for your Mac. You can add more if you like. At the bottom of the window, you can set how the Tab key works. Either Text boxes and lists or All controls.

Print and Fax Pane:

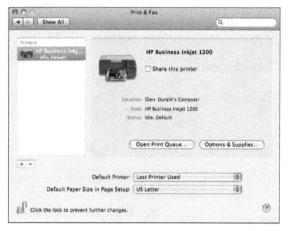

I have a small in-depth section on printing later on. But, here is the basic Print & Fax Pane. Notice that I have one printer and it is not shared. The default Paper Size for Page Setup (in an application) is also set here.

Sound Pane:

There are three main windows in the Sound Pane. To the right is the **Sound Effects** window. Here you can choose your favorite alert sound, set the alert volume and how it is played, set your output volume (mute if you like also) and finally, if you want to have the volume option in your menu bar.

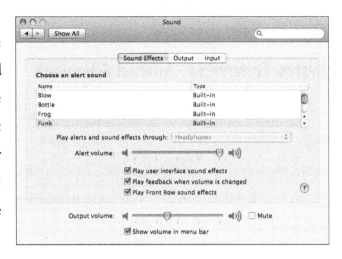

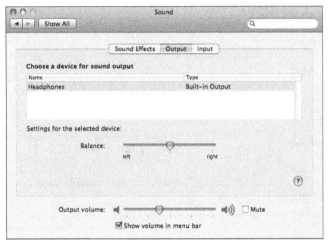

The next is **Output**.

Here you can choose your output device. I have an attached set of speakers plugged into my headphone jack. You can also set the balance and output volume here as well.

Input is the last option. I do not have a microphone attached so I have not inputs.

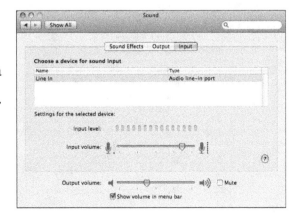

The input level "graph" would show the loudness of the audio coming in. You can also adjust the Input volume.

System Preferences - Internet & Network

Need to get online to search for information on a subject or the latest news on your favorite sports team? These preferences are key to getting you there. I am attached via a cable modem (Ethernet plugged into Mac) and I have wireless access for my laptop. I will go over each window to help you understand what goes where and what info you need to get online.

MobileMe Pane:

MobileMe is a service that Apple provides that easily allows you to perform some tasks for your Mac. You can backup files, access your Mac from another location....

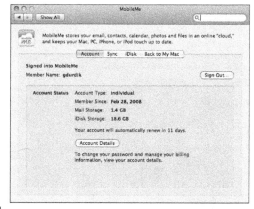

Is it worth it? It has its pros and cons, but with the latest version and 10.5 it has gotten a lot nicer. I go into further detail later on in the guide.

Network Pane:

First - notice **Location:** at the top of the window. If you travel and use a laptop, you can save the necessary settings for each location. On the left – you see the three Interfaces: Ethernet, Airport and Firewire.

Note that both Ethernet and Airport are connected at this time. You can easily tell this because there is a Green button next to each. Notice that the Firewire interface is not connected at all and has a Red button next to it. If you have a Yellow button next to any of the options then the connection is only partly good. Further investigation is needed to see why this is not a solid connection.

Assist me...

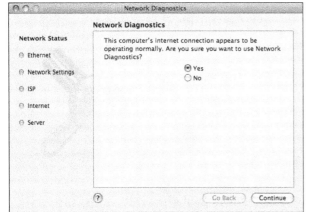

If you are having problems getting online, this button gives you two choices to help figure out what is wrong. The first is **Network Diagnostics**. Notice on the left that all of the steps that could have a problem are OK. All options have a Green button next to it. If you click on Continue, your Mac will go through its testing procedure.

The second is – **Network Setup Assistant**. This will guide you through the process of communicating with your service provider and get your Mac configured for them.

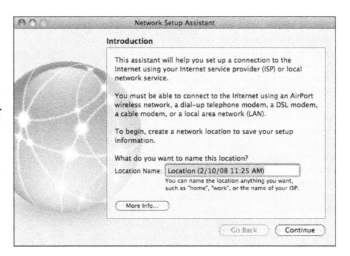

Advanced Button:

You may or may not ever have to access this option. But, there are lot settings here that can

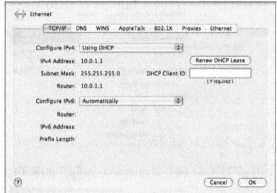

be configured. One common example is adding a Proxy Server. This will prevent unwanted material from getting to your Mac. The first is TCP/IP. Note that I am connected via DHCP. Every device must have it's own unique address. A DHCP server hands out the address to your computer. If you choose a

static address, you must know its IP address, subnet mask and router info.

DNS:

Again, you probably will never have to configure this if you are a home user.

WINS:

If your Mac connects to a Windows computer, here is where you input the necessary settings.

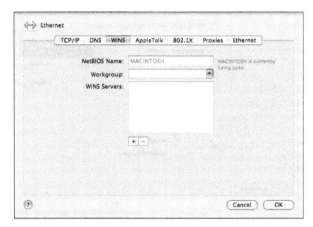

AppleTalk:

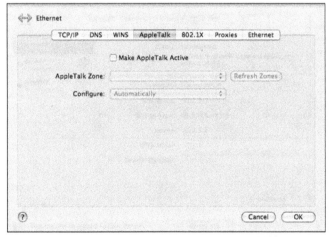

AppleTalk is a way that Apple invented a long time ago to easily connect networkable devices. It is really not needed anymore and should remain off.

802.1X:

This protocol and its settings are used for wireless networks. This is shown below.

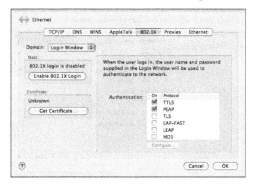

Proxies:

Note on the left that you can enter in a Proxy Setting for numerous protocols. Web Proxy is for the Internet for example.

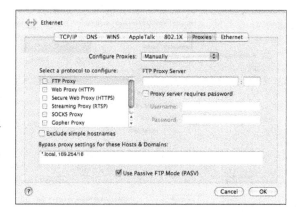

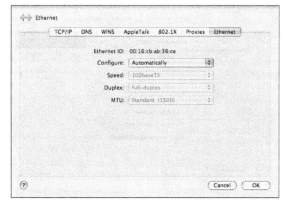

Ethernet:

Again, you probably will never have to access this window. Just note that it does show you your Ethernet ID (every device is unique) and the speed of your connection.

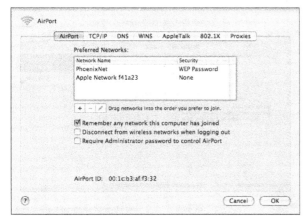

Airport – Advanced Tab:

This is similar to the Ethernet Advanced tab. You are also given the choice to remember any network joined, disconnect from wireless networks when you log out and require an Admin password to control Airport.

QuickTime Pane:

QuickTime is a technology for playing audio and viewing video files. It is in this pane that you can configure its settings. The first is the **Register** window. This is shown to the right. Note that I am registered as a Pro User. (QuickTime Pro icon on the left of the window – Pro would be left out if I was not registered) If you purchase this option, you are given

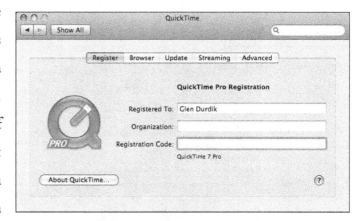

more options for playback and can save movies. I took out the registration code to not make it available to other users.

The next screen is **Browser**. Here you are given the option to automatically play movies as they are downloaded and to save the movies in disk cache. This will make playback later on faster.

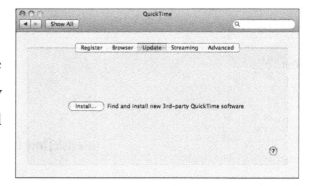

The next screen is called **Update**. Here you can find new third party "enhancements" to QuickTime and install them.

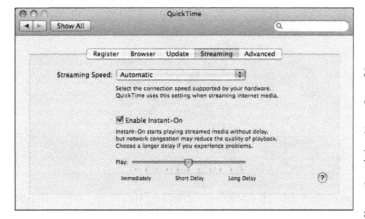

Streaming allows setting the connection speed for streaming media. Automatic does this for you. **Enable Instant-on** determines the time it takes to start playing streaming media. In the example to above – it is set to Short Delay.

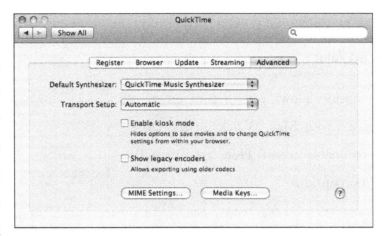

Advanced - This option does not get accessed that often. The first two settings can be left alone. **Enable kiosk mode** hides options to save movies and changes QuickTime settings from within your browser.

MIME Settings can be useful if you encounter playback problems. This window is shown below. It allows you to specify what type of files QuickTime will open.

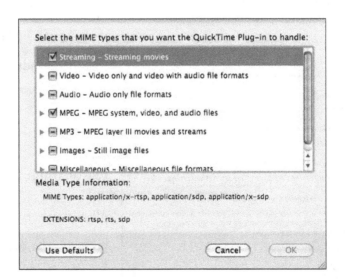

Sharing Pane:

This option allows you to turn on or off access to your Mac. Click on the empty box to enable access. Here are just a few common options.

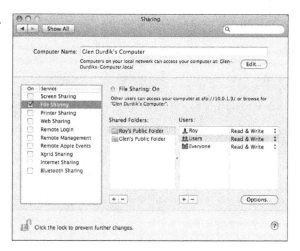

Screen Sharing:

☐ Anyone may request permission to control screen

☐ VNC viewers may control screen with password: _____

(Cancel) (OK)

options shown above.

Allows others to remotely view you Mac. If you click on Computer Settings... you get the

File Sharing:

Allows others to access shared folders. Here are the key windows for it.

File Sharing – Options Window. AFP is the default setting to share files. You can also use FTP (File Transfer Protocol) or SMB (Windows). Notice that it states these last two options are not fully secure.

System Preferences – System

Accounts Pane:

When you first setup your computer, you create one user – the default Administrator account.   If you want to create new accounts (one for each co-worker or child for example) this is where you do it. Notice that there are four accounts. My account is the active account. Underneath the account name is the type of account it is. For this example, there are two admin accounts (Roy and Glen) and one standard account (Junior). I clicked on Junior. Since he  is not an admin account – the options for his account are as follows: Reset Password, Allow user to administer this computer, and enable Parental Controls. Parental controls will be discussed later as it is a separate pane. If you click on Login Options, you are given the screen to the right. **Automatic Login:** If you disable it, the default account will be logged on. Below this option, are the two choices if you do not select Auto login. They are **display login window as a list of users** or **type in the**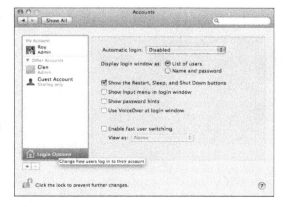

username and password. Also, you can decide if you want to **show the restart, Sleep and Shutdown buttons, show input menu in login window, show password hints** or use **Voiceover to speak the options available.** The last option here **enables or disables fast user switching.** If enabled, you do not have to logout in order to get to another account.

Additional Options for active accounts: Roy is the current user in the example to the left.

Login items are little applications that run as soon as you login. Sometimes, these could cause a problem. Just click on the box next to the item to activate or deactivate it. If you want to add more, click on the plus sign towards the bottom of the window.

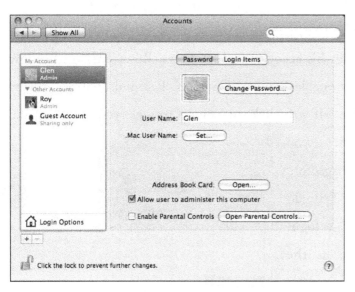

The other option is **Password.** Notice that you can change your password (screen on next page), set your .Mac User name, allow this user to administer this computer and enable Parental Controls. As Glen (in this case) is an administrator, it would not make sense to enable the Parental Control restrictions.

Change Password Screen – For changing each account's password.

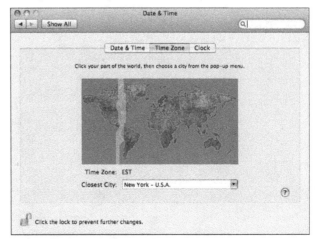

Date and Time Pane:

This pane is divided into three different windows. The first is **Date and Time**. This is shown to the left. The first option – **Set date and time automatically** (Server Name) will constantly check your time and correct it if it is different from the specified server. You can also change the Date (on the left) and the Time (on the right). Notice that the setting to change date and time formats is found in the International Pane. I discussed this pane earlier in the manual.

The next option is **Time Zone**. Click on the globe shown in the middle of the screen on the closest (you can get) to your city. I live in NYC and New York is on the list of available cities.

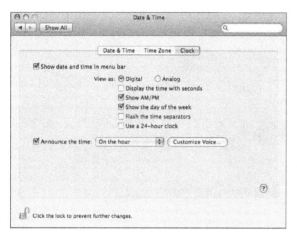

The last option in this pane is **Clock**. The first choice is how you want the clock in your menu bar to be shown. You can also have your Mac announce the time at specified interval. Customize voice will let you select the voice of your choice.

Parental Controls Pane:

There are a lot of settings in this pane. You can lock down an account for very limited access for a young child or give many rights to a more experienced & trusted user. There are four main categories and Log window. The four categories are: **System** (shown below), **Content**, **Mail & iChat** and **Time Limits**.

System:

The first choice is whether or not you want the user to **use a Simple Finder**. This uses a smaller dock, no items on the desktop and less menu choices.

The second option is (if checked off) what can be used applications. Notice in my example that all are available except for iTunes. At the bottom of the screen are four more choices. If the user can administer printers, they have access to adding or deleting printers. The next option allows you decide whether or not the user can burn CDs or DVDs. The third choice will give the user the option to change their password. The last option can give the user to modify the dock.

Content:

This gives you the option to hide profanity in the Dictionary application and determine what type of website restrictions you want for that user.

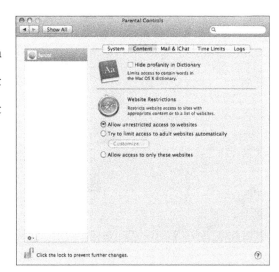

Mail & iChat.

This window gives you two choices. To limit a user to a certain list of email addresses or iChat sessions.

Time Limits:

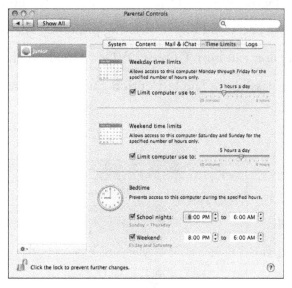

There are three main options in this window. The first two determine how many hours the selected user can use your Macintosh. It is broken down into weekdays and weekends. The third option allows you to set specific times when the user CANNOT use the computer.

Logs:

This gives you the ability to trace all activity by the selected user. It is broken down into the

following categories: Websites Visited, Websites Blocked, Applications and iChat. You can also set the time interval you want to see.

Speech Pane:

This pane has two main options. They are Speech Recognition and Text to Speech.

Speech Recognition:

The main option located on the top of the screen is turning Speakable items on or off. You

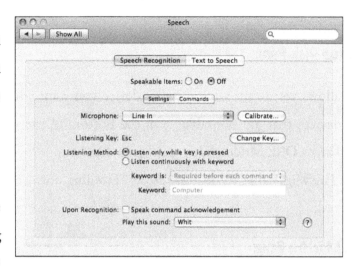

can also choose what key to press to activate the Listening mode for speech recognition or set it to continuous with a keyword. Last, you can set your Mac to signal you that the command received by playing a sound that you choose.

Text to Speech:

There are several options in this window. The first, at the top of the screen allows you to set

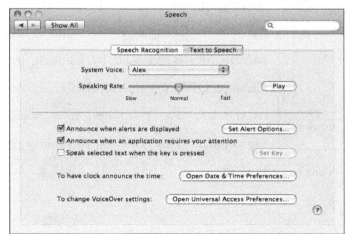

the **System Voice** and it **Speaking Rate**. Click on play to test the settings and try all the voices. Next, you can have your Mac speak alerts, announce a problem with an application, speak selected text when clicking on user defined keyboard key or keyboard combination. The last two options link back to the Date & Time preference for announcing the time and the Universal Access preference to set VoiceOver settings.

Startup Disk Pane:

This allows you to set what drive or device you want your Mac to boot from. It will show only devices that are bootable. On the bottom of the window, you can restart your Mac into Target Disk Mode. This turns your Mac into a regular external hard drive. You must use a FireWire cable to do this. Note: Holding down the T key while restarting does the same task.

Time Machine Pane:

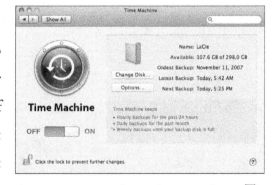

Time Machine is Apple's easy to use backup software. Whether you hard drive crashes or you delete a file by accident – having a copy of that file or drive will save the day. The first window gives you three options. The most

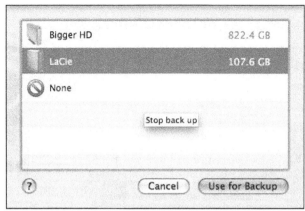

important option is turning Time Machine **ON** or **OFF**. This is done by clicking on the slider on the left side of the screen. Changing the location of the backup files is accessed by Clicking on **Change Disk….** This option is shown to the left. The third option is called **Options….** This gives you the ability to decide what hard drives you DO NOT want to be backed up.

This window is shown to the right. Notice that you can have Time Machine warn you when old backups are deleted.

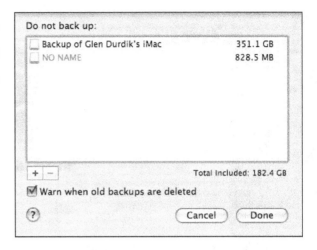

Time Machine Application in Use

(Time Machine Dock Icon)

OK. Something really bad happened and you think all of your hard work is now GONE. Time Machine to the Rescue!!!! If you click on the Time Machine icon in your dock...the screen below is what you will get. Let me point out the key items in this Application.

Today (Now) - This is the status of the backups at this moment in time.

Arrows Pointing towards the back of the window and pointing to you – This is the way you navigate between backup intervals.

Time Line on the Right of the screen – This is a visual guide to the date of the backups

Restore – This will recover the file or files that you need to get back from the *eternal* trash can in the sky.

Time Line Interval Expanded – Notice that the bars get larger as you move over the date you select. I have my cursor on Sunday, November 11, 2007 and it is the largest bar.

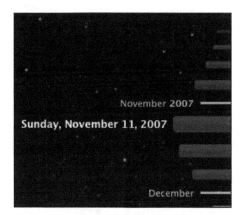

Example of window of previous backup – Notice that the date of the backup is shown at the bottom of the screen.

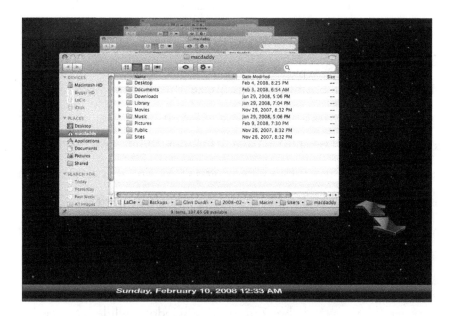

Universal Access Pane:

This preference gives you the option to provide visual or audible assistance when using your Macintosh. It is broken down into five segments. The first is **Seeing**. This is shown to the right. **VoiceOver** is the first option. With it on, most of the mouse actions you take will result in a voice stating what is being done. This does NOT read your text back to you. If you click on **Open VoiceOver Utility...**, this

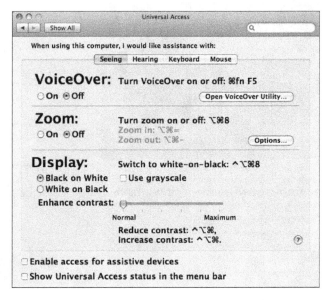

application is run and gives you several options to customize this feature. The second option is **Zoom.** In short, this will expand the size of a selected area. You can choose **Options** to change the default settings. The third setting is **Display**. Here you can use the default setting of Black text on white or use the inverse or grayscale. You can also enhance the contrast. The fourth item allows you to **Enable access for assistance devices**. The last option lets you decide whether or not you want access to Universal Access status to be

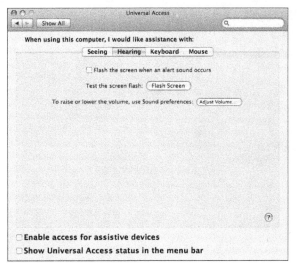

shown in the menu bar or not. These last two options appear in every choice at the bottom of the window while configuring Universal Access.

The **Hearing** option gives you the ability to have your Mac Flash the screen whenever there is an alert.

Next, the **Keyboard** preference gives you a variety of choices to modify how typing on your keyboard works. The first choice deals problem of typing more than one key at a time. The second category deals with problems typing (need to type slow) or typing repeated keystrokes.

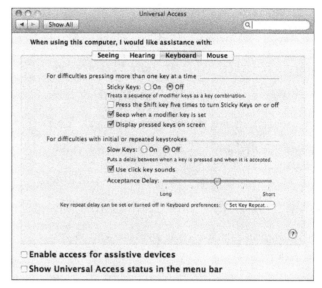

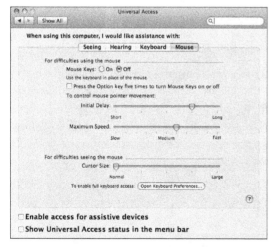

Last is the **Mouse** preference. The first option is to allow the keyboard to replace the mouse functionality. You can also configure the mouse pointer movement (Initial Delay and Maximum Speed of the mouse). The last option is to change the size of the cursor.

Setting up a USB Printer in a Flash (well quickly anyway)

OS X version 10.5 differs from previous version in regard to setting up a printer. As most users have a USB printer, I will primarily go over setting one up in the next few pages. The first step is to access your **System Preferences**. Once this is open, click on the **Print & Fax** option located in the Hardware section. You will then be shown the screen to the right. Notice that there are no printers available currently. You also can choose what the default paper size is for your printer and if you

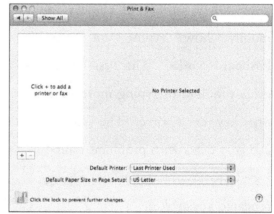

have more than one printer – what the default printer would be. Unlock the system preference if it requires it. Next, click in the plus sign (+) towards the bottom left of the window.

Note: OS X has many printer drivers already installed. However, you may have to install the

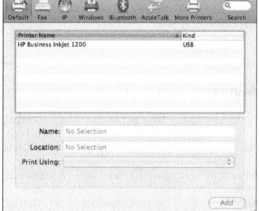

drivers from the manufacturer's CD that came with the printer. In the example I am using, the Mac recognized the Printer Model and that it is attached via USB.

When the install process is complete – you can name the printer, where it is located and the Mac states what driver it is using for the printer. Last, click on Add and the printer is installed on your Mac. I have an additional software package to create PDFs – that is the Adobe PDF 8.0 option in the window. Note: OS X can print any document to a PDF just by clicking on the PDF option when printing.

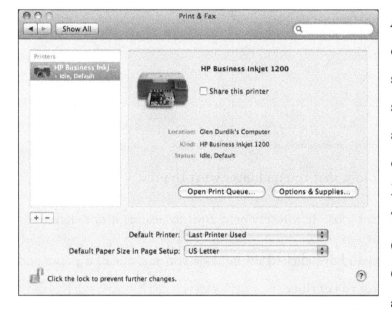

After the printer setup is complete – you will now see the screen to left. Notice that it states it is IDLE (not in use) and is the default printer. You can also share it with other Macs attached to the network. The other two options are **Open Print Queue...** and **Options & Supplies**. **Options and Supplies** gives you the option to change the name and location, driver info and (if supported) Supply Levels.

Print Queue Window (click on Open Print Queue)

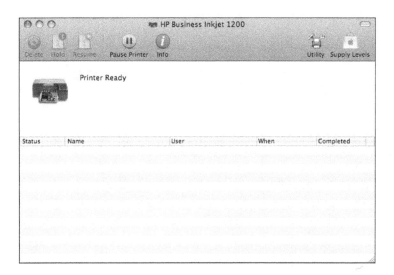

Delete – Allows you to delete print jobs that you no longer what to print.

Hold – Allows you to hold your print jobs. It will stay held until to resume it or delete it.

Resume – Resumes printing after you have clicked on hold or you ran out of a paper and just added more and what the printer to continue.

Pause Printer – Again, this pauses all printing. (Note – feature does not work on my HP printer – therefore it may not work on your USB printer as well)

Utility – Brings up the manufacturers software to manage the printer. In my case, it one feature it brings up is the ink status of the printer. Remember, this was not available through the Supply Levels section discussed earlier.

Supply Levels – If supported shows you the status of the ink and other consumables.

Side Note – IP Printing. (If you have your own small network in your house)

Protocol – Depending on how you are recommended to install it, you have a few different Protocol choices. They are **Internet Printing Protocol (IPP)**, **Line Printer Daemon (LPD)** and in my case **HP Jet direct Socket**.

Address – Every device on a network has it's own "address." If you access the Internet through a service provider – you are usually given an address via their DHCP server. In other words, you cannot give you Macintosh a permanent or "static" IP address. You can, however, give your printer a static address. I just put 10.0.0.1 as an example address.

Queue – You can name the print queue in this option.

Name – You can name your device here.

Location – If you choose, you can state where the printer is located. (bedroom, office, den, etc.)

Print Using - You may have to manually select what driver your printer uses.

Mac OS X Utilities - The Basics

There are many utilities to help configure your Mac or resolve a problem you are having. They are located inside the Application folder of your hard drive. The Utility folder icon is shown above. Depending on what type of user you are, you might use most or just a few of these utilities. I will describe each and go into further detail on ones that you should know how to use. Note: Disk Utility is VERY important to know. I cover this utility at the end of this section.

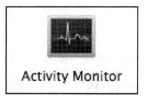

This utility allows you to see what is going on "under the hood" of your Mac. In the example below, I chose to show System Memory. You can also choose CPU usage, Disk Activity, Disk Usage and Network statistics. On the upper right of the screen, there is a red

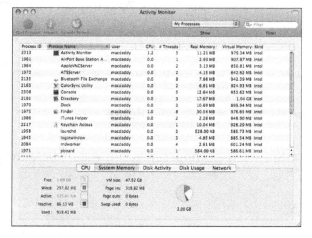

STOP sign. If you click on a process that you want to quit (perhaps an application not responding) and click on the STOP sign – the process will be turned off.

Airport Utility is used to configure Apple's wireless solution. Discussed in detail form pages 85 - 92 in the manual.

Use this setup utility to setup audio input and output devices. You devices must be connected and all necessary software installed as well.

Allows you to easily transfer files via Bluetooth to a Bluetooth capable device. (Your Mac must have Bluetooth capability also)

Boot Camp Assistant

Boot Camp Assistant allows you to install the Windows operating system on a separate hard disk partition. You need to have Windows software, 10.5, and enough hard drive for the hard drive partition this utility creates. Note: You boot into Windows – you will have no access Macintosh functionality. You need to purchase a virtualization software package to have both available at the same time. I discuss this application later on in the manual.

ColorSync Utility

Your monitor should have a "ColorSync" profile for it installed on your Mac (you may have to install it yourself). This utility allows you the works with these profiles. As a regular user – you probably will never have to access this utility.

Console

This utility displays all "log" files generated by you Mac. Normally, you would not have to use this utility. However, if something is consistently going wrong, this utility might show you what is not loading or having issues. A sample screen is shown on the next page.

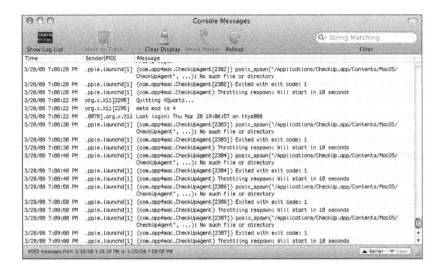

This utility – when launched – will show you the exact percentages of R (red) G (green) and B (blue) of the item your cursor is over. Good for reproducing color in documents.

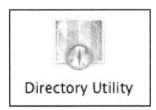

This utility is used when you are attached to OS X servers. Not in use otherwise.

This is used in conjunction with the utility above. It allows you to scan for users among other things.

This is the one utility EVERY Mac user should know how to use. I will cover this utility in detail at the end of this section.

This utility allows you to take a screen shot of a selection, window, screen or perform a timed screen capture. If you launch this utility, these items are under the Capture menu.

Grapher

This utility allows you to visualize 2D and 3D equations. One of the sample 3D equations is shown below.

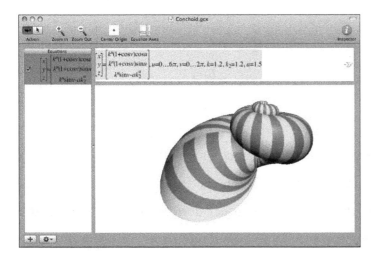

Keychain Access

This utility stores all of your system (and others you allow to add to it) passwords.

Migration Assistant

This is most commonly used when you want to transfer items or clone your old Mac to a new one.

Network Utility

This is a very useful utility. It gives you access to many common IP tools. In the example below, I am using the PING command. Every device on the Internet has its own unique address. To test if your Mac is "getting out" and see other devices, the Ping command is perfect. All it does it take an address you type in and try to get to it. If it gets through – then things should be all right. If it fails, maybe your Internet service is having network issues. **Note:** In example below it states **100% packet loss**. This means it could NOT get to the device I requested.

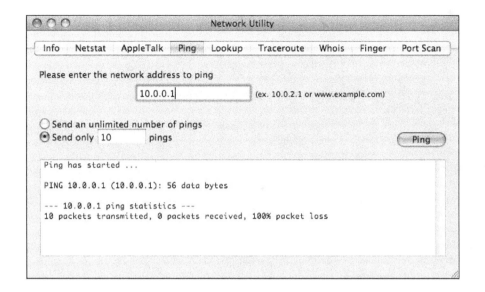

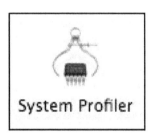

System Profiler

This utility gives you all the specifics of your computer. Look here if you are unsure of what hardware is installed on you Mac. Below is a sample screen. Note all of the choices under **Hardware** and there are options for **Network** and **Software** as well.

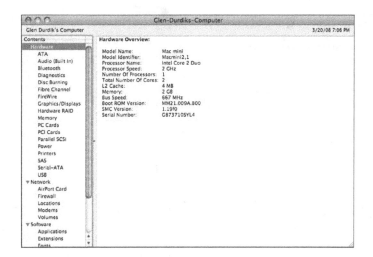

Mac OS X is based on UNIX. The GUI (graphical user interface) is applied over the UNIX shell so that most users will not have to learn or use UNIX commands. However, it maybe useful to learn a few and the Terminal is place to access UNIX directly.

This utility configures all aspects of the VoiceOver application. Below is the screen to adjust Navigation settings.

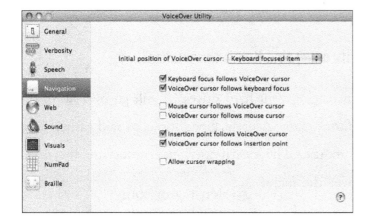

This is a utility to access special version of UNIX called X11. Most users will not have to use this environment.

Disk Utility – To verify or repair... that is the question?

Disk Utility is very useful for managing your hard drives. I will go over all of the options in this utility. Disk Utility performs many different functions. I as said earlier, a lot of these any user should know how to use. The casual user may never use the other functions. The next few pages goes over the major features and where they are located.

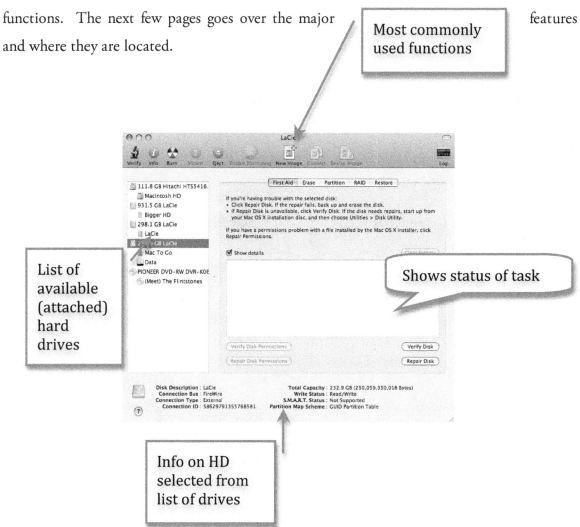

Most commonly used functions

List of available (attached) hard drives

Shows status of task

Info on HD selected from list of drives

Verify:

Checks various structures of the hard drive (not user-changeable) to make sure the hard drive is healthy or needs repairs. You can also access this by clicking on the Verify Disk button on the bottom right of the window. An example of what this checks is shown below.

Info:

Gives you all the details of the hard drive you have selected.

Burn:

Allows you to burn to a disk an "image" of your choosing.

Unmount/Mount:

Your hard drives are only available if they are "mounted." If you want to remove a disk from your Mac – then choose unmount. You can also drag a hard drive to the trash can to perform the same task.

Eject:

Removes the CD/DVD from your optical drive.

Enable Journaling:

New Image/Convert/Resize Image:

These three items deal with "images." An image is a file created by a user that converts the

contents of a hard drive to a format that usually is smaller in size and able to be read/converted back by any Mac. To the right is an example of the option available when creating a new image.

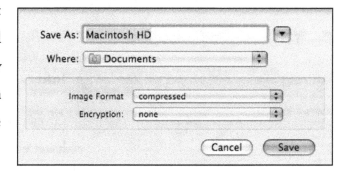

Log:

Shows all of the tasks that Disk Utility has performed over a period of time.

First Aid:

This tab includes four categories:

Verify Disk Permissions: Unix creates permissions for all files on your hard drive. Sometimes, they get corrupt and can cause problems. If you choose, Verify Disk Permissions, the utility will find, if any, problems, but will not fix them.

Repair Disk Permissions: This tab will fix any errors found on the hard drive. A sample of verify permissions is shown below.

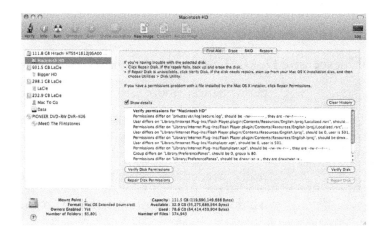

Verify Disk: Checks the hard drive for certain types of errors that could cause problems for the Mac. A sample window is shown earlier under the Verify option.

Repair Disk: Hopefully, if problems are found, this function can repair the damage. If you run Verify Disk or Repair Disk and it states it CANNOT fix the problem, then a major disk error has occurred. If you have third party utilities, you might be able to resolve the problem. **This is the main reason backup software like Time Machine is mandatory.**

Erase:

This is where you format a hard drive or flash drive. You can choose a variety of formats, but **Mac OS Extended (Journaled)** is the default and should be used in most cases. You can also name the device, erase Free Space and change security settings. This tab is shown to the right.

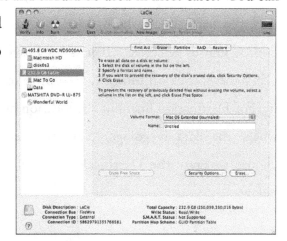

RAID:

RAID stands for Redundant Arrays of Inexpensive Disks. This feature was meant to increase

performance, more storage space and reliability. It is useful for several types of work done on your Mac, but is not really needed for a casual user. The window for this option is shown to the left.

Restore:

This involves images or an actual hard drive. In the **Source** line, you select what you want copied over. In the case below, a chose the hard drive "Macintosh HD." Just drag the name of the hard drive into the Source line to select it. If it is an image ON a drive, click on **Image...** to browse to it. For Destination line, put the location of where the data is going. You can also

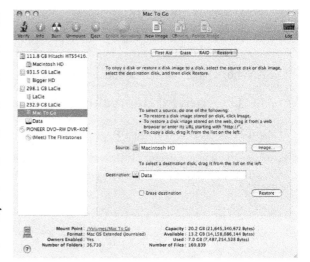

choose to **Erase the Destination** before the Restore is performed. This option is shown below.

Airport Utility

Below is an example of a fully configured Time Capsule. Notice on the left of the screen is the name of the device – Phoenix Net and that there is a green light next to the name. This means the device is on and fully functional (network access).

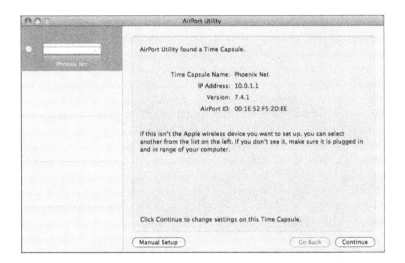

In the middle of the screen – you are given some basic info on the device. On the bottom left is the Manual Setup button and on the bottom right – Continue. If you click on Continue, you will be given a choice at every screen that follows to keep the settings your configured on the screen or to modify them. As this is a device already configured – I will continue this guide with screenshots of a Manual Setup. This will begin on the next page.

You will notice that there are five different groups of settings – Airport, Internet, Printers, Disks and Advanced. To the right is the first screen you will see if you click on Airport. This is called the **Summary** tab and info shown here - can not be modified at this screen.

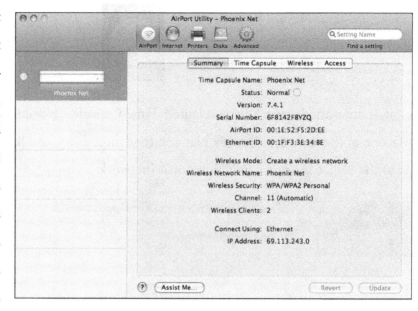

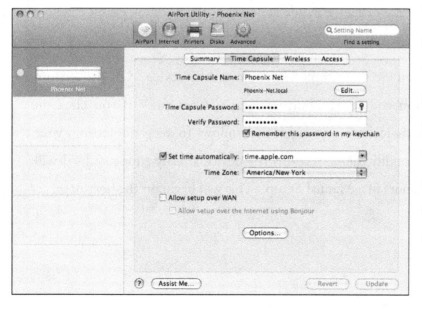

The **Time Capsule** tab is shown to the left. Here is where you would change the name of the device, change the password of the device, set the time and time zone and allow the device to be configured over the network (WAN).

Next is the **Wireless** tab. Wireless mode gives you to the choice a regular wireless network, participate in a WDS network (group of devices acting as one) or extend an existing

network. Here you will name your network, determine the radio mode (N and B/G compatible or different types of N only), the channel (automatic should be good for most users), wireless security (you can choose none, but this is not recommended), and last

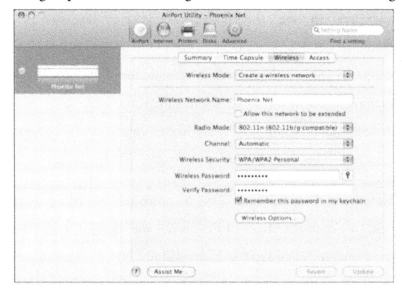

your password. Towards the bottom of the screen is **Wireless Options**. This is shown abovce. The only two options that you might need to use are "**Create a closed network**" and "**Use interference robustness.**" If you create a closed network – a user must also know the name of the network as is it not displayed. Interference robustness helps to clear up some static caused by a cordless phone for example.

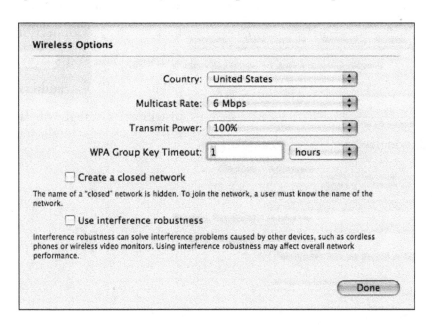

Access Tab - One way to further increase security is to ONLY allow certain MAC addresses to see the network. ALL computers and network devices each have a unique MAC address. You could for example enter in the MAC address for your desktop and laptop and only these two devices will be able to use your network.

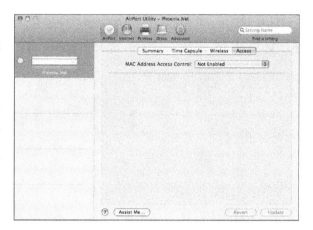

Next is the **Internet** tab. This is shown below. Most users will keep the Ethernet option next to Connect Using. PPPoE is not the used for most consumer use. This also applies to the Configure IPv4 setting. Most will use DHCP – not manual. Next is the Ethernet WAN Port. You might have to configure this setting as the devices you connect to Airport might need a speed locked in. Automatic is good for most devices. Last, is Connection Sharing. You can share a public IP address, distribute a range of IP addresses or OFF (Bridged mode).

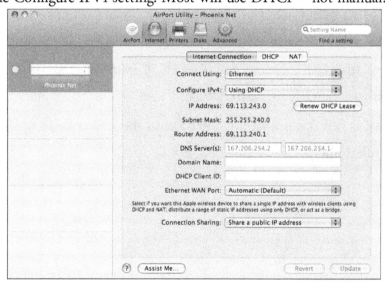

To the right is the **DHCP** window found in the Internet tab. As a consumer, you probably will never have to use this.

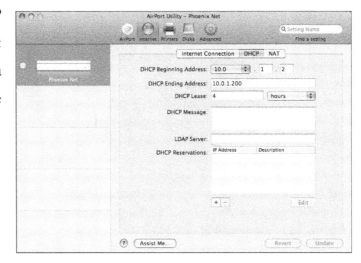

Last is the **NAT** window. Again, the default settings should be fine for most consumer applications.

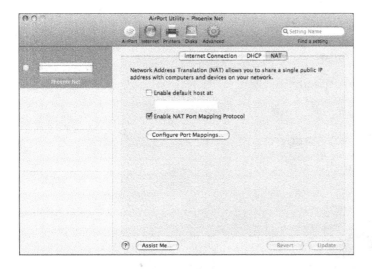

The **Printers** Tab is next. Basically, if you connect a USB printer to your Airport, you can have all users have access to it. This screen is shown below.

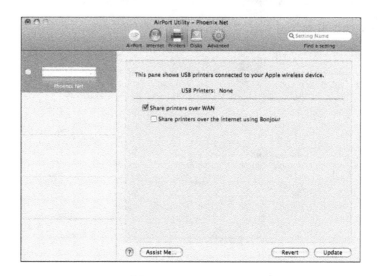

Next is the **Disks** Tab. The first screen is the **Disks** Window. This is shown to the right. Her you see a list of all available Airports and the capacity of the device. You can Archive your device or erase it here. If you want to unplug the device, you can disconnect all users.

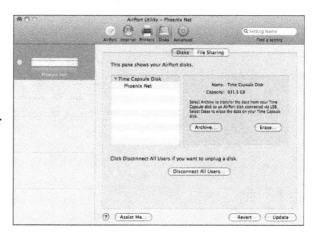

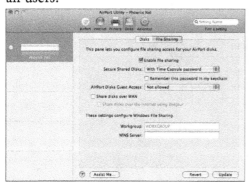

The second window is **File Sharing.** You set the Airport to share storage devices attached to the

Airport. If you select Share disks over WAN, you then have the ability to share the disks over the Internet.

The last tab is **Advanced**. Most of the items here may not be useful to you, but I will show you all of them so that you know where they are found. The first window is **Statistics**.

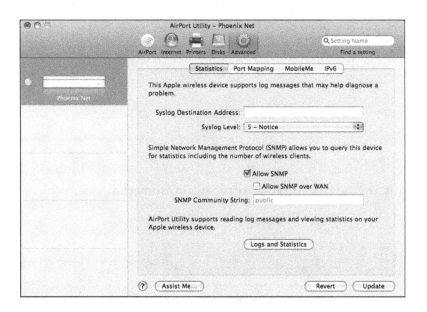

The next is **Port Mapping**. Different network services are sent on different ports. (File Sharing or FTP for example.) This window allows you to set access via your Airport.

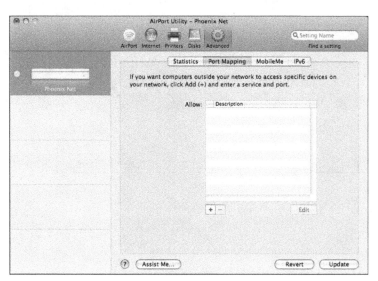

The next window is **MobileMe**. The primary goal of this window is activate the Back to My Mac feature of MobileMe.

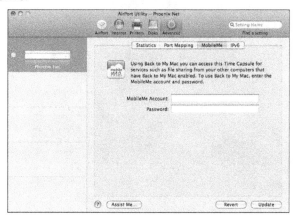

The last option is the Advanced tab is **IPv6**. Again, something you probably don't have to worry about.

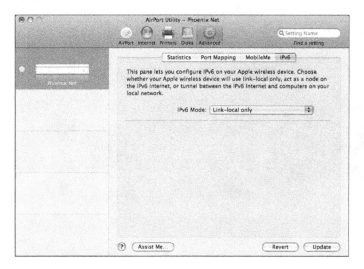

In Brief - Mail.app

Click on this to receive new mail.

Deletes email and puts into trash. Only after deleting from trash is it really gone.

Mail has a spam filter that removes "junk" from your inbox. Use this to change an email to "Not Junk or Junk."

Mailboxes
(Here there are two. A .Mac account and another one called Road Runner).

List of emails in the folder you are accessing – (Trash in this example)

Window showing actual contents of emails.

Create a new email.

Reply – sends email back to sender, Reply All – sends email to all recipients of the then mail, Forward – allows you to send the received email to new individuals.

Search Mail for an item in various ways.

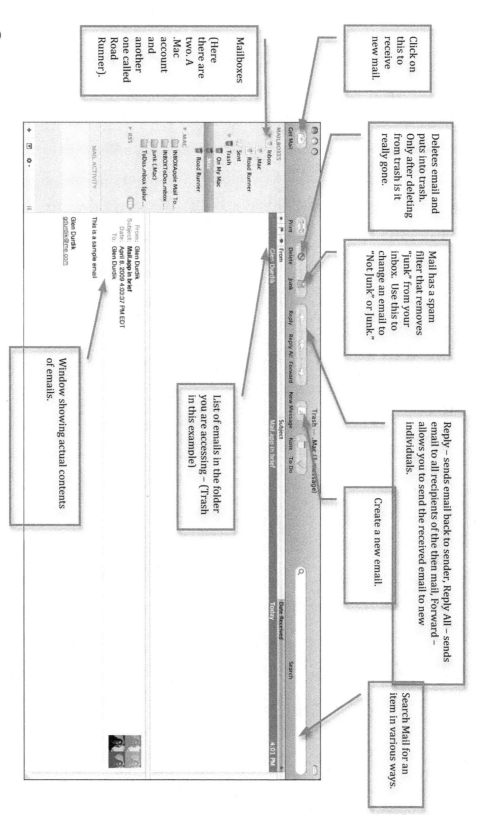

Mail.app is included with all versions of OS X. There are a lot little details to go over to understand the full power and ease of use of Mail.app. I just want to go over the key points in this guide to get you on the road to email nirvana. On the previous page is a sample window of the program. I highlighted the key aspects of the window and left out other more advanced or not important in daily use. Mailboxes are where the email you receive is stored. You can have as many mailboxes or email accounts as you want. There will be a number next to the Mailbox and in the dock icon for Mail.app if there are any new messages when you are accessing the program. If you network connection is down, you will see a warning sign next to the Mailbox name. There are a lot of choices to search in Mail.app. Below shows an example of a search for "email." Notice you can select **All Mailboxes**, just the one you are in, the **Entire Message**, the **FROM** line, **TO** line or the **SUBJECT** line.

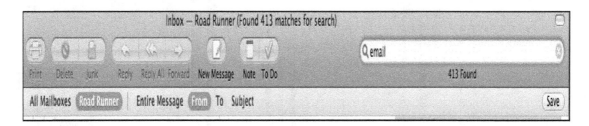

Setting Up a New Account

When you first start Mail.app, you are asked to create a new account. This account will be then given a Mailbox name. Notice in the example to the right – that there is an option to Automatically set up an account. If this fails, you are given the choice to manually insert the settings needed.

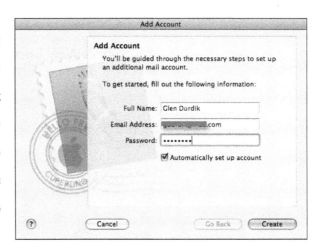

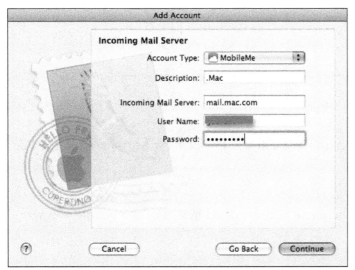

The first setup screen is shown to the left. First, you must know what type of account it is. The choices are shown below.

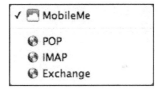

MobileMe is a paid service from Apple. Most email accounts are POP accounts. Some work environments will use Exchange. What you enter for the description will become the name of the Mailbox. Next, you must know the Incoming Mail Server. Please find out from you Internet provider or company what has to be put in this line. After this, enter in your User Name. This is the part that goes before the "@" sign in your email address. So, my email address is (blocked out by black line) (username) @mac.com. Last enter in your password. In a later window, you must also know the Outgoing Mail Server.

Sample New Email Window

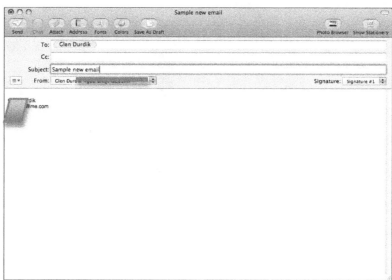

If you click on the New Message button on the main window or New Message from the File Menu...you get the above screen.

To: This is where you insert the email address or addresses of the people you want to send the email to.

CC: Used to send email to secondary people.

Subject: This is where you briefly tell the recipient what the email is about. It is recommended – NOT to leave this blank.

From: (Glen Durdik in the above example) This sets what account you are sending it from. If you only use this program for one account – then there will not be any choices available.

Signature: In Mail.app – as with other email programs you can setup what is called a "Signature." Notice in my example I have chosen "Signature #1." Therefore, whenever I create a new email, my name and email address will appear at the bottom of my email.

 This button gives you the option to add additional items to your New Message Window. This dialog box is shown to the right.

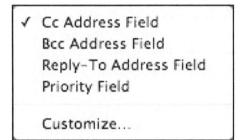

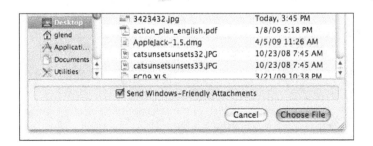 The Attach button allows you to add – "attach" items to your email. Note: There maybe a limit set by your provider as to what the maximum size is of an email. Note: If you are sending an email to a Windows User – please remember to check off – **Send Windows – Friendly Attachments** in the dialog box.

One cool item is Stationary. You can have one of wide selection of backgrounds for you email. In the example below – there are five choices for a Birthday email. Announcements, Photos, Stationary and Sentiments are you other choices. You can drag items you plan to use regularly to the Favorites section.

Well, those are some of the highlights of Mail.app. You can start using it and gradually learn more as you go on. I want to keep this brief, but I decided to add just the screenshot of all the menus so that you know where to look for other items.

Mail.app Menus

Mail.app Menu

About Mail – Tells you what version you are running.

Preferences – This menu option brings up the window shown below the first screenshot to the left. It includes editing accounts, setting up Junk mail and creating signatures to name a few.

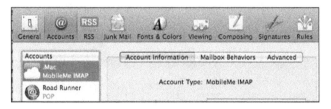

New Message	⌘N
New Note	^⌘N
New To Do	⌥⌘Y
New Viewer Window	⌥⌘N
Open Message	⌘O
Close	⌘W
Save	⌘S
Save As...	⇧⌘S
Save as Stationery...	
Attach File...	⇧⌘A
Save Attachments...	
Quick Look Attachments...	⌘Y
Add Account...	
Import Mailboxes...	
Add RSS Feeds...	
Print...	⌘P

File Menu

Here you can create **New Messages, notes or To Dos.** You can also bring up the default window again by choosing new Viewer Window.

You can attach files, save attachments or do a "quick look" which previews the contents. You can add accounts or import Mailboxes from Entourage, Netscape, Eudora, Mail for Mac OS X or mbox files. Last you can add RSS feeds or print your email.

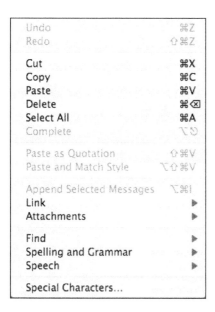

Edit Menu

Here you can undo or redo the last action you took, use cut, copy and paste, set the rule for incoming attachments, access the find feature, Spelling and Grammar tools, activate the Speech feature and have you email read to you and finally Special Characters.

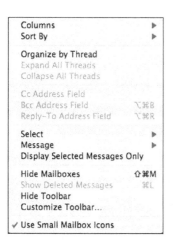

View Menu

Here you can set what is to be shown in the columns found in the Viewer window. You can also decide how you what you mail to be sorted (date received or from for example). You can select all messages in thread and hide the Mailboxes from the default viewer.

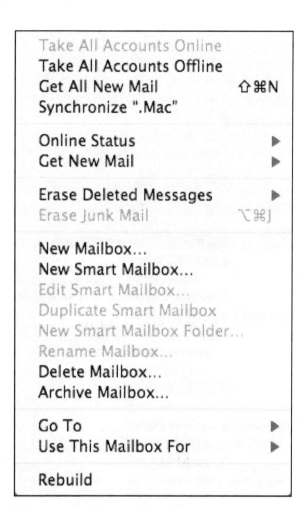

Mailbox Menu

In this menu, you can disable accounts by taking then offline or enabling them by taking them online. You can check the online status of your mailboxes and get new mail here as well. You can erase deleted messages from one account or all. You can create new mailbox or smart mailbox (mailbox that contains emails from other locations that you specify). You can delete or archive mailboxes. You can go to various folders such as the **Inbox** or **Trash**. Last, you can rebuild you email by re-downloading your emails from the server.

Send Again	⇧⌘D
Reply	⌘R
Reply All	⇧⌘R
Reply With iChat	⇧⌘I
Forward	⇧⌘F
Forward as Attachment	
Redirect	⇧⌘E
Bounce	⇧⌘B
Mark	▶
Move To	▶
Copy To	▶
Move Again	⌥⌘T
Apply Rules	⌥⌘L
Add Sender to Address Book	⇧⌘Y
Remove Attachments	
Text Encoding	▶

Message Menu

In this menu you can send a message again, reply or reply all, forward or forward as attachment, redirect an email bounce it, mark is as unread, flagged or junk and set its priority. You can copy or move emails, apply rules and add the sender of an email to the application called Address Book. Last you can remove attachments from an email and set what text encoding you want to use – it is set to automatic.

Show Fonts	⌘T
Show Colors	⇧⌘C
Lists	▶
Style	▶
Alignment	▶
Indentation	▶
Quote Level	▶
Make Rich Text	⇧⌘T

Format Menu

In this menu you can show fonts and colors, how you what to specify a new list in your email to look, change the style and alignment of text and last increase or decrease the indentation or quote level.

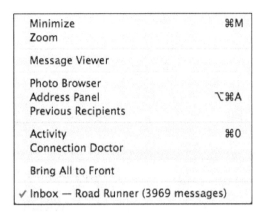

Window Menu

Her you can minimize a window to the dock, zoom the page to it greatest size for the screen, access the Message Viewer, photo browser, address panel, a list or previous recipients. The Connection Doctor window is shown to the left. Note – Green dot – account OK. Red dot – account access not going through.

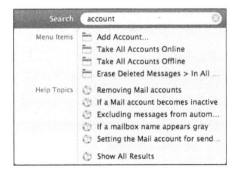

Help Menu

I just covered all the basics to get started using this great program. Please come here for future problems or topics you want to learn more about. In the example to the left – I did a search for "account."

In Brief - Boot Camp Assistant

Boot Camp Assistant

With the arrival of the Intel processors in Macs – Macs can now run Windows natively. There are a few programs that run Windows in a virtual environment while the Mac OS is running. These are not free, but are useful and quite popular with users. Bootcamp Assistant is an application that takes a part of your hard drive and installs Windows on it. **Note: You have to restart and hold down the OPTION key to decide what OS you want to use – Windows or Mac.** Why chose this? The Mac is running as a dedicated Windows machine and all devices attached should play nicer when the Mac is in the native Windows mode. So, if you need Windows with special devices – Bootcamp is probably your best option. It is really simple to get this process rolling. The first thing to do is to locate the application - which is found in the Utilities Folder located in the Applications folder. The icon is shown at the top of the page.

The first screen is shown to the right. Note that you can print a complete Install and Setup guide by clicking on the **Print Installation & Setup Guide button**.

Next, click on continue. This brings up the required partitioning

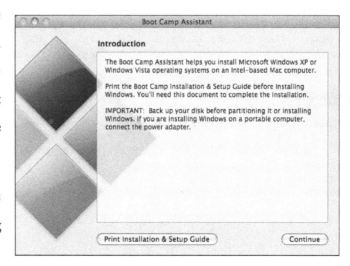

of your hard drive. Most users will keep a large section dedicated the awesome Macintosh

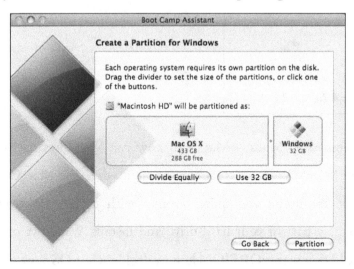

OS and keep a smaller one for Windows. In the example shown to the left, I decided to use the default 32 GB size. This should be fine for most users. If you intend to do a lot of video work, music downloads, gaming – a larger size might be better for you.

Last Mac step is simple – just click on Start Installation. Oh, put in your Windows OS disk

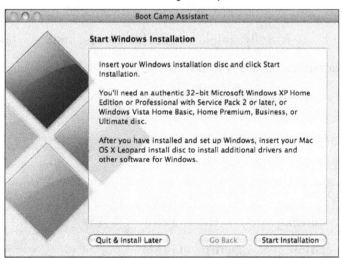

first – then click on the button. Your Mac will restart and for better or for worse – Windows will start its thing and start installing whatever version of Windows you are installing. I have one note – I was installing Vista and the partition the Mac formatted did NOT work with it. I had to reformat it during the Windows setup screen so that Vista can work on it. Interesting.

Have fun running Windows. At least it is running on great hardware.

A few notes on other Mac OS included software.

The Mac OS comes with a bunch of included software to do various things. I discussed Mail.app, Bootcamp Assistant and later on (most users get) iLife (part of the Complete Guide or available to purchase separately. I just wanted add some thoughts on a few other applications.

Address Book -

This is not your Father's Address Book. I bring this up to show one of 10.5's cool features. Data detectors. But first, you agree that the sample window to the right is very

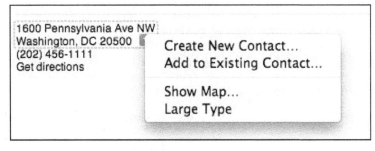

straightforward. But let's say you get an email with and new or updated address or new contact or phone number. Enter in Data Detectors. So, let's say I just got an email with address of the White

House – not sure why, but I had to chose something. Move you mouse of the address in the email. Notice that the address is now highlighted and there is a down arrow on the bottom right of the address. The Mac recognized this an address and if you click on that arrow – ask you what you want to do with it. Viola!! You can add it to your Address Book – or show it on a map. I think this a great feature.

Font Book -

Font Book is a great way to sample fonts found on your Mac. The main window is shown below.

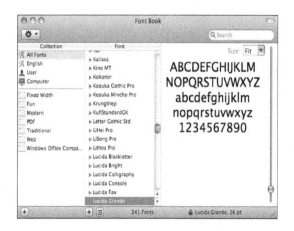

Nice. But what if you want to add fonts or disable them? This is where to go. Oh, you can also validate fonts – they do get corrupt from time to time. Anyway, go to the File Menu and the option to add a font or disable/remove a font is found here.

New Collection	⌘N
New Library	⌥⌘N
Add Fonts...	⌘O
Close	⌘W
Save Report...	⌘S
Validate Font	
Validate File...	
Delete "All Fonts"	
Remove "Lucida Grande" family	
Export Fonts...	
Reveal in Finder	⌘R
Print...	⌘P

Note that you can print the sample here as well. Go to a Mac Software Update site – mentioned later in the manual and download a program or two that will print page after page with more than one font per page. If you just got a Mac – VERY USEFUL.

iCal -

iCal is you guessed it – a calendar. Nothing really too new here. I sample calendar is shown below.

But...if you are a user always on the go and need to access you calendar at anytime where there is a computer – then getting MobileMe is worth it. You can publish you calendar and have MobileMe always keeping it up to date. Go to the Calendar Menu and chose Publish. This is shown on the next page.

Photo Booth

The majority of Macs now have a built-in camera. You can use this for video chat and in the case oh Photo Booth – take pictures or a movie clip.

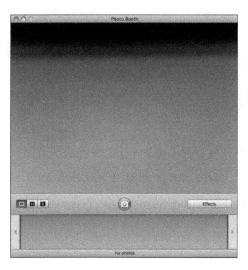

The Photo Booth main window. (Camera Image Blocked)

Takes one picture.

Takes a series of FOUR pictures.

Takes a video.

Click on this button to take the picture(s) and start and stop a video capture.

You can apply a lot of cools effects and backgrounds to your photo or video. Below is just the first group of choices.

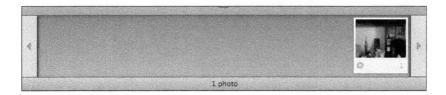

If you take a photo or video they appear in the "Gallery" below the main window.

If you click on the picture – notice what choices now appear above the gallery. You can email the photo or video, send it to iPhoto, make it your account picture or as your buddy picture for iChat.

Ports on a Typical New Mac

There are a variety of ports on the back (or front) of your Mac. I just wanted to show what each looked like and what they do. Each has a unique icon over the port to tell you want it is.

The port with the Headphone picture is for Audio out. Connect you computer speakers or headphones to this port.

The port with has two triangles going into a circle is for a microphone.

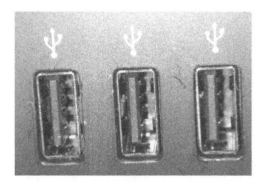

The three ports above are all USB ports. On newer Macs these are 2.0 ports. They also can use the older standard as well. You can recognize them by the three lines coming out of a small dot. Keyboards, mice, scanners, external hard drives mostly use this type of port.

This is a FireWire 400 port. Most Macs have this port on them. It is ideal for attaching a video camera or other video devices. You can tell that it is a FireWire port by the picture that shows a circle with three items coming out of it. Two of them are two small lines and the third is a thick square.

This is also a FireWire port. However, it is a FireWire 800 port. This is much newer than the older 400 type. Again, it is used for more high-end applications like video editing. More and more external hard drives have this port on them now.

This is your Ethernet port. This is what connects you to a network or the Internet if you do not have wireless access on you Mac. It looks like a phone jack, but it is not. You can tell it also by the two arrows pointing in different directions with three dots in the middle.

This is the external video port on a more recent iMac. If you have a different model or laptop – this port will look different.

Apple is adopting a Mini Display port on newer models. This is shown below.

On laptops, there is a special power connector called a MagSafe Connector. This is shown below.

Useful Keyboard Commands (start to become a Power User)

Command Key = ⌘ = Button on both sides of your Spacebar

⌘ + C	Copies the items you have selected.
⌘ + V	Pastes the last item you copied into your current document.
⌘ + X	Deletes whatever you have selected.
⌘ + A	Selects the whole contents of your open document. (good if you want to change the font or font size to everything)
⌘ + Z	Undos your last action.
⌘ + F	Brings up the Find Feature.
⌘ + S	Brings up the Save Dialog window if saving for the first time. Next use will just save over older version.
⌘ + SHIFT + S	Brings up the Save As Dialog window.
⌘ + P	Brings up the Print Dialog window.
⌘ + Q	Mac asks you if want to quit the application

	you are currently using.
⌘ + W	Closes your current window.
⌘ + OPTION + W	Closes all windows
⌘ + N	In application – New Document. In Finder – Opens up a new Finder Window.
⌘ + SHIFT + N	In Finder – creates a New Folder.
⌘ + O	Opens a file, folder or application
⌘ + I	Allows you to Get Info and any item (size for example)
⌘ + E	Ejects the selected item (CD for example) and removes it from your Mac.
⌘ + DELETE	Moves the selected item to the Trash Can. (Not deleted until you empty the trash)
⌘ + SHIFT + DELETE	Tells the Mac to empty the Trash Can.
⌘ + SHIFT + OPTION + DELETE	Tells the Mac to empty the Trash Can = WITHOUT THE WARNING. (Use only when you are 100% sure you know what you

	want to delete.)
⌘ + 1	In the finder, this makes the current window into the ICON view.
⌘ + 2	In the finder, this makes the current window into the LIST view.
⌘ + 3	In the finder, this makes the current window into the COLUMN view.
⌘ + L	Makes an Alias (Shortcut) of the selected item.
⌘ + R	Shows the original file or folder of the alias you chose.
⌘ + D	Duplicates the file or folder you have selected.
⌘ + M	Minimizes the current window.
⌘ + OPTION + M	Minimizes ALL windows.
⌘ + ?	Opens Mac Help or the Help Menu for the application you are currently in.
⌘ + SPACEBAR	Opens the Spotlight application to do a

	quick search of your hard drive.
⌘ + OPTION + D	Shows or Hides the Dock
⌘ + TAB	Switch between open applications.
OPTION + DRAG	Copy to a new location.
⌘ + DRAG	Moves the selected item to the new location – without copying.
⌘ + SHIFT + 3	Allows you to take a picture of your screen.
⌘ SHIFT + 4	Allows you take choose a selection of you computer screen.
⌘ SHIFT + 4 , then SPACEBAR	Allows you to take picture of the selected window.
⌘ + OPTION + ESC	Allows you to FORCE QUIT an application. (For example, you see a rotating "beach ball" that never stops spinning_
CONTROL + EJECT	Brings up the Restart, Sleep or Shutdown dialog box.
⌘ + SHIFT + Q	Brings up the LOGOUT dialog box.
⌘ + SHIFT + OPTION + Q	Logs you out immediately

<u>Special Modes of OS X</u>

Pressing "C" at startup.	Tells your Mac to boot from the inserted CD or DVD that has a valid System Folder. (Keep track of you install disks so that you can perform key utilities while booted from it.)
Press "T" at startup.	Tells your Mac to boot a FireWire device and nothing more. (Good if you want to copy files to and from several Macs.)
Press "SHIFT" during startup.	Tells your Mac to boot into SAFE BOOT MODE. This temporarily disables unneeded system items and login items. (If encounter certain problems – this is a good way to rule out or discover what could be giving your Mac grief.)
⌘ + V during startup.	Tells your Mac to boot into Verbose Mode. (Another diagnostic tool to try)
⌘ + S during startup	Tells your Mac to go into Single-User Mode. (Useful if you are familiar with basic or advanced UNIX commands to help resolve

issues or modify settings.)

General Tips to Keep You and Your beloved Mac in tip-top shape

Any computer is a complex device. It needs to be maintained just like a cars should. Follow these suggestions and keep your Mac humming along with nary a crash.

1. **By Virus Software.** Yes. There are Mac viruses out there and there are bound to be more. Be safe and invest in one. This applies also to your Windows environment. If you have Windows running on a Mac – **GET VIRUS Software NOW**. (Both for the Mac and Windows version you are running.)

2. **Backup.** A hard drive is a mechanical device. It has a lifecycle – so it could die from a defect in a few months or just die from wearing out. I recommend buying an external hard drive that is at least or – greater in size then the hard drive in your Mac for backup purposes. **Time Machine** – part of OS X.5 is simple and east to setup with the external drive. Note that there are third party backup software that have more options and features than Time Machine.

3. **Whenever Apple comes out with a system update (10.5.5 to 10.5.6) download and install the COMBO Updater.** This is usually a larger file than what is downloaded by Software Update. Many people believe this process decreases the chance of issues arising after the update is applied. I never really never had a problem - but if others say it is better – Be Safe. Also – **BACKUP your drive** and **Repair permissions** before an update is performed.

4. **Keep the System Disk that came with your Mac or a store bought copy of OS X.5 handy at all times.** If something does go wrong – you can check permissions

and the state of the hard drive by running Disk Utility on the CD. I covered this is detail in an earlier section.

5. **Recommendations for Mac use:**

    a. **Keep your desktop clean and uncluttered.** The Mac treats every icon on your desktop as a separate window which will COULD slow down Mac operations. It is easy to place things there – but organize the items and take them off ASAP.

    b. **Make sure your Mac has a lot of extra hard drive space.** The Mac needs this space to create temporary files when it is doing its thing. Little space – less breathing room – could cause issues. Some applications also require more than others – graphic art programs for example require more.

    c. **Create a "Dummy " account on your Mac with admin rights.** If something goes wacky with an application – log into this test account and try the application again. If it works – you know it is that account and not the Mac or software.

6. If you are having problems with a specific program – try step C above. If it works – then a Preference file in that account can be corrupt. Your preferences are located in your hard drive -- Users Folder -- Your Account Folder (Its icon is a small house) -- Library Folder (has Library icon in folder) -- Preferences. The Preference usually starts with COM, the software vendor (APPLE or ADOBE), the application it is used for (AddressBook, Dock, Photoshop) and PLIST. If iCal is not working correctly, then you would navigate to the Preferences folder and drag **com.apple.iCal.plist** out of this folder and try it again to see if now works.

7. **You can try running in SAFE mode to see if this fixes the problem.** Hold down the SHIFT key when rebooting to enter this mode. It disables many things that MIGHT be the issue. This includes running only Apple installed startup items,

disables all fonts except for those in the SYSTEM folder, disables login items and trashes all font caches.

8. **Try booting in Single User Mode.** Restart and hold down the Command and S keys until a black screen with text appears. When this is done type **fsck –y**

   This runs a File System Check. If after it is run it states items were modified – the Mac tried to fix an issue with your system.

9. Mac takes time for itself. While you are sleeping dreaming of the new iPod coming out – the Mac is running scripts that perform maintenance to the System. I put my Mac to sleep at night and let it do its thing. Some people turn off their Mac….save energy - but scripts are not being run daily. Therefore, you can go to one of the Mac software sites I mention and search for utilities that perform these CRON SCRIPTS at any time you want.

Useful websites for Macintosh Users

Apple daily News Sites

www.macobserver.com

www.macintouch.com

www.macnn.com

www.macdailynews.com

www.macsimumnews.com

www.macworld.com

www.maclife.com

Sites to find updates to software or locate software you might need

www.versiontracker.com

www.macupdate.com

Sites to find Apple and Mac OS tips

http://www.apple.com/pro/tips/

http://www.macosxtips.co.uk/

http://www.mactips.org/

http://www.macworld.com/article/134859/2008/08/leopard_tips.html

http://www.macworld.com/article/61203/2007/11/more105tips.html

<u>Need to know what might be out in three months?</u>

<u>www.macrumors.com</u>

<u>www.appleinsider.com</u>

<u>Show your Apple pride and purchase massive quantities of Apple Merchandise!!</u>

<u>www.missingbite.com</u>

<u>www.redlightrunner.com</u>

MobileMe

MobilMe is a very, very useful set of tools for some people. For many, its features are nice,

but not 100% critical for everyday use. I want to go over the key features of MobileMe – and let you decide if the fee is worth it. The first place to go is the MobileMe system pane located in the System preferences. Notice it the example to the right that I am already signed in and I am accessing the **Account** tab. Here is gives me some basic facts about my account

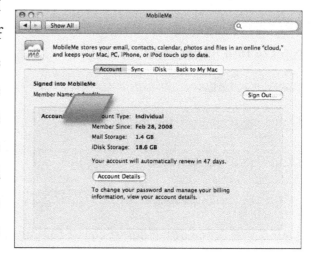

– the most useful telling me how much disk storage I have left in my iDisk. You also have a link called Account Details that bring up a webpage with more specific info.

The next tab is called **Sync**. This is one feature that is very handy if you have access to more than one Mac on a daily basis. Basically, it monitors the settings you select and makes sure than when you change it on one Mac – it will be there on another Mac. Note: You have to be signed in under your own account on whatever Mac you want to use this on. Currently, in the example

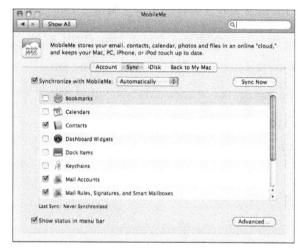

above – I am not syncing (item has to be checked off) all the items available for syncing.

The next tab is called **iDisk**. This is another really nice feature. Think of it as a spare hard drive that is always available when you can log into MobileMe. In the example to the left –

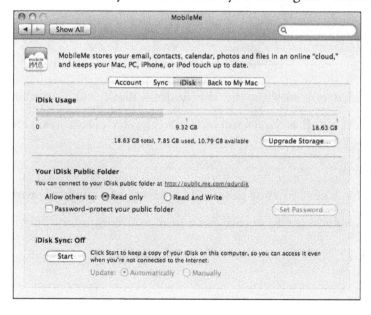

notice there is a status bar telling me how much space I used and that I can upgrade my space if I desire. You can also setup access to a "Public" folder which means it could be accessed by individuals besides you. I recommend setting a password (not done in example to the left). Last, you can set up iDisk to keep a copy of the contents on your hard drive as well. If you do this, you have the option to automatically have it updated when changes to iDisk are made.

The next tab is **Back to My Mac**. This allows to access you home Mac from a remote location. Note: Depending on the setup of either Mac – network settings configured by your company or ISP may block this feature.

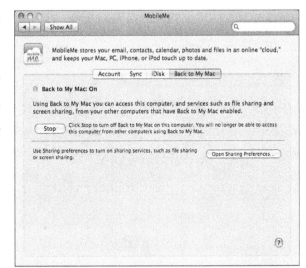

MobileMe – The Internet Connection

If you goto www.me.com, you can access many of MobileMe's useful features. The first is having access to your email account. This is shown below.

The next two options which I decided not to show are the Address Book and Calendar. Bascially, if setup, you can have access to all of your contacts and calendar events available when logged into www.me.com.

The next item (flower icon) gives you access to your gallery. This serves as a place to store photo albums and videos that you might want to access away from you computer. This is shown on the next page.

The next feature is again iDisk. Here you can access to files anywhere you can login. This is shown below.

One feature that was just implemented is the ability to share large files through your iDisk feature. Most Internet providers put a cap as to the size of the file that can be attached to an email. With this new feature – you send an email with a direct link to the file. Large file – no longer a problem.

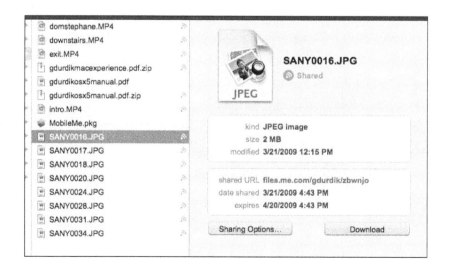

To do this, highlight the item you want to be shared and click on Sharing Options. This brings up the next window, which is shown below.

Here, enter in the mail address or addresses of the people you want to send the file too, enter a message, state how long the link to the file will last and finally, decide if you want to give the file a password for access. Click on Share to make it so or Stop sharing to end the sharing of the file.

The last item is the **Account** tab. This gives you the complete details of your account. This is shown below.

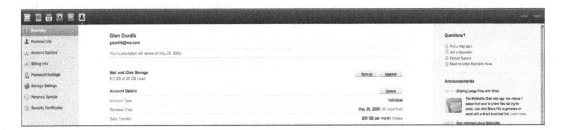

So is MobileMe for you? It has a few items that many will use. It has some – that many wont use. Oh, I forgot one thing…you get an email account that ends in ME.COM. I think that most people have a few email addresses already – so that is not critical. I do LOVE sharing large files and having the ability to create a web gallery of not just photos, but videos as well. Note: One option is to allow viewers the ability to download your photos and videos as well. Nice.

Almost Forgot - Safari 4.0

Safari is Apple's own web browser. It is familiar to anyone who has used a web browser before to surf the Internet. I would like to go over the interface and basic features of this piece of software. Below is a screenshot of the default window of Safari.

 This allows you to go forward or backward in terms of the websites you visit.

This is the Home button. You can specify in Safari to always go to a default web address and this button returns you this website whenever you wish.

This button allows you to add a bookmark of the current site to Safari. Bookmarks are necessary as websites can have large urls and be difficult to remember. If you have a lot of favorites, having this allows you to keep them and be organized.

This is the place to enter in the address of the website you want to visit – it's URL. This website has a RSS feed (news summaries) and therefore has access to it with RSS icon in this window. The arrow going in a circle is the reload button. If a site is having trouble loading, reloading my reset the connection and load faster. Maybe.

This is an easy way to access the Google search engine. The looking glass icon gives you access to recent searches.

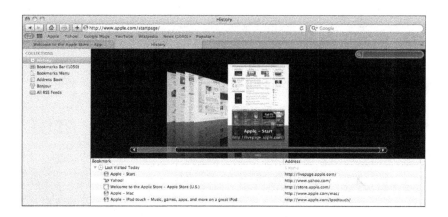 This button brings up a list of all of your bookmarks on the left side of your browser screen. This is shown below.

This button brings up a nice new feature called Top Sites. An example of what comes up is shown below. I small snapshot of the site is shown – just click on the one you want to bring to a full screen. On the bottom right – is a Search History window.

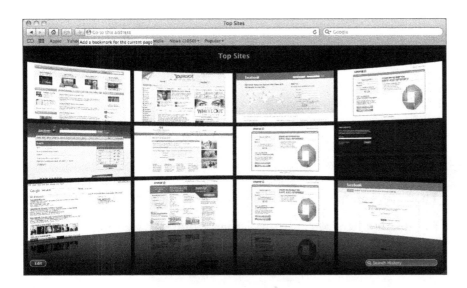

The Menus of Safari 4.0

Safari Menu

About Safari – tells you what version you are running.

Preferences are shown on the next page.

About Safari	
Report Bugs to Apple...	
Preferences...	⌘,
✓ Block Pop-Up Windows	⇧⌘K
Private Browsing...	
Reset Safari...	
Empty Cache...	⌥⌘E
Services	▶
Hide Safari	⌘H
Hide Others	⌥⌘H
Show All	
Quit Safari	⌘Q

Safari Preferences - General

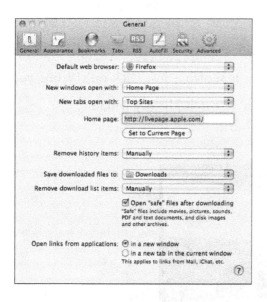

Default web browser: – There are a number of web browsers for the Mac. Here you choose what browser you want to launch when you open link that requires a website. Here it is Firefox.

New windows open with: - Determines how a new window opens. It could be your Home Page, Top Sites, Empty Page, the Same Page and few other choices.

New tabs open with: Basically, the same options as a new window.

Home Page: - This is where you enter in a new default website. Below is the button to click if you want the page you are currently on to be the Home Page.

Remove History Items: – The History contains a list of all the site you have visited. You might want to remove this for various reasons and this preference allows you to set how it is treated.

Save downloaded files to: - The default is the desktop. This is OK, but remember having a zillion icons on your desktop slows down your Mac.

Remove download list items: Default is manual. It can also be when you quit Safari or upon a completed download. Below is a check box if you want Safari to open "Safe" files automatically. This means it should be safe from viruses. Remember it is good to purchase an anti-virus software package –just to be 100% safe and sound.

Open links from applications (like Mail or Entourage): It can be in a new window or a new tab.

Safari Preferences – Appearance

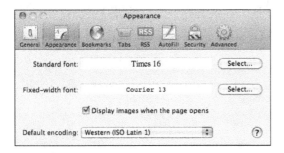

Unless you have a problem with the way Safari looks and feels – you probably won't use this preference.

Safari Preferences – Bookmarks

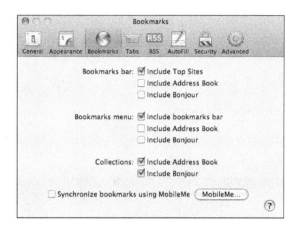

Here you can have Top Sites, Address Book and Bonjour available in the Bookmarks bar and or the Bookmarks menu. You can also synchronize bookmarks using you MobileMe account. So, you can login to MobileMe on any Mac and click this option and wham-o all you bookmarks are available to you wherever you are!!

Safari Preferences – Tabs

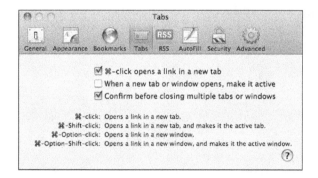

This gives you a few settings for tabs in Safari. Note: The keyboard combinations listed here to have quicker and easier access to tabs.

Safari Preferences - RSS

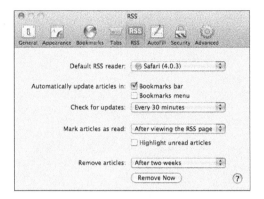

RSS is a cool way to access news from various sites. This window gives you several options to customize how Safari treats RSS feeds.

Safari Preferences - AutoFill

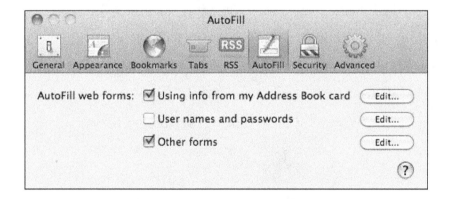

If you want Safari to automatically put in your name and address info whenever you need it in a website – this is where you configure your settings.

Safari Preferences – Security

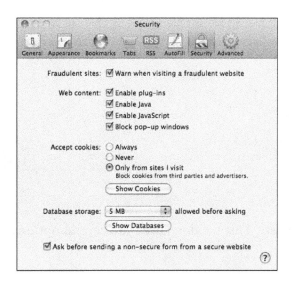

This is an important preference. Fraudulent sites – warns you if it is troublesome site. Web content: - Each of the checked-off items shown above could in some way be dangerous. Nothing out there yet to worry about though. Accept cookies: - Cookies are little items that most websites use when you visit them. The default is - Only from sites I visit. Others will not be used. This is probably the best choice to use. The - Ask before sending a non-secure item…. – is important as you want all vital personal information to be sent as safely as possible.

Safari Preferences – Advanced

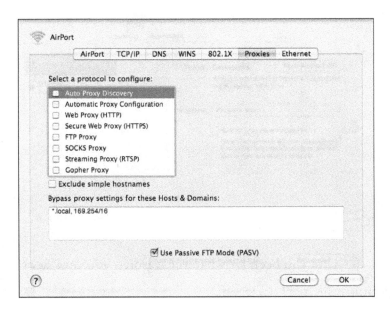

These settings are again – not used on a daily basis. Universal Access is Apple's technology for users who have difficulty with the default interface of Safari or the OS as well.

However, if you are in an organization, you might need to enter in a few security settings to "get out on the Internet." Click on the Change Settings button next to Proxies to access these settings. The window it brings up is shown below.

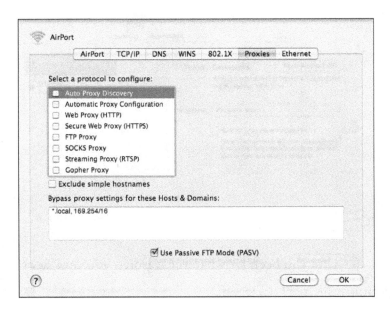

Private Browsing

Read the above screenshot – it pretty much explains what it does – good if you don't want anyone seeing where you were on the Internet.

Reset Safari

If you want to remove any evidence of where you been for whatever reason – you can choose what you want to get rid of. By default – all are checked off.

Empty Cache

A "cache" is data stored by a web browser to help speed access to that website the next time you visit it. Here is where you can delete the cache stored by Safari.

Safari – File Menu

New Window	⌘N
New Tab	⌘T
Open File...	⌘O
Open Location...	⌘L
Close Window	⇧⌘W
Close Tab	
Save As...	⇧⌘S
Mail Contents of This Page	⌘I
Mail Link to This Page	⇧⌘I
Open in Dashboard...	
Import Bookmarks...	
Export Bookmarks...	
Print...	⌘P

This menu is pretty straight-forward. I just want to point out Open in Dashboard. This allows you to create Dashboard widget for the item you select in the webpage. An example is shown below.

Safari – Edit Menu

Undo Remove Bookmark	⌘Z
Redo	⇧⌘Z
Cut	⌘X
Copy	⌘C
Paste	⌘V
Paste and Match Style	⌥⇧⌘V
Delete	
Select All	⌘A
AutoFill Form	⇧⌘A
Find	▶
Spelling and Grammar	▶
Special Characters...	⌥⌘T

This menu is also pretty simple. Basic options. Here is where you find – the FIND command for Safari. Great if you want to search a page for a word of interest.

Safari – View Menu

Hide Bookmarks Bar	⇧⌘B
Show Status Bar	⌘/
Show Tab Bar	⇧⌘T
Hide Toolbar	⌘|
Customize Toolbar...	
Stop	⌘.
Reload Page	⌘R
Actual Size	⌘0
Zoom In	⌘+
Zoom Out	⌘–
Zoom Text Only	
View Source	⌥⌘U
Text Encoding	▶

This menu determines what is shown on the screen in the browser. You can also Zoom IN and Zoom out of the page. The items you can put in the Toolbar is shown on the next a page. To access this feature - choose Customize Toolbar... shown below.

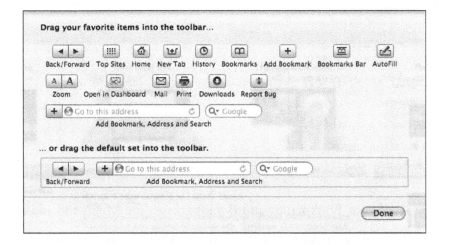

Safari – History Menu

Show Top Sites	⇧⌘1
Back	⌘[
Forward	⌘]
Home	⇧⌘H
Search Results SnapBack	⌥⌘S
Reopen Last Closed Window	
Reopen All Windows from Last Session	
☐ Welcome to the Apple Store – Apple Store (U.S.)	
⊘ Apple – Mac	
⊘ Apple – iPod touch – Music, ga...ps, and more on a great iPod.	
Show All History	
Clear History	

Here you can see the Top Sites (shown previously), go forward or back through sites visited, go back to your Home Page or show the complete History by selecting Show All History. You can also delete the History of sites visited here as well.

Safari – Bookmarks Menu

Show All Bookmarks	⌥⌘B
Add Bookmark to Menu	⇧⌘D
Add Bookmark for These Tabs...	
Add Bookmark Folder	⇧⌘N
▦ Bookmarks Bar (1050)	▶

This menu allows you to see all of your Bookmarks, add Bookmarks to the Menu and add a Bookmark Folder. A folder is useful to organize the many sites I am sure you are going to visit. I have one for all the Macintosh sites I visit on daily basis.

Safari – Window Menu

Here you can Zoom (make bigger) or Minimize (window shrinks down to go into the Dock), keystrokes to access Tabs, view you Downloads or Activity. Bring All to Front – takes all of your open Safari windows and puts them on top of any other application window you have open.

Safari – Help Menu

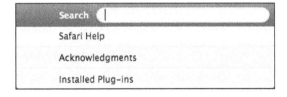

Here you can search for Help on items found in Safari. This menu will also give you a very useful list of Installed Plug-ins. These are enhancements to the basic feature set of Safari.

Summary of features new to 10.6 and other tidbits

10.6 a.k.a Snow Leopard is an evolutionary step forward to the Mac OS. Much of the interface is unchanged from 10.5. Snow Leopard is a leap forward in the background processes. The Finder was rewritten and this OS only runs on Macs equipped with Intel processors. There are a lot of little items that were tweaked alongside some more interesting ones that I will discuss here. There is a great – extensive online article that goes over extensive detail what is new and changed. It is found on the Macintouch website. Before you upgrade – this site also has a super list of what software packages work and which need to be fixed. This website is constantly updated. If you go to this website – please support them and help allow these very useful sites stay up and running. You can go to their website and use their link to Amazon for example. You pay nothing, but they get a small fee from this.

Note: ALWAYS backup your hard drive before doing a major upgrade or a minor one (10.6 to 10.6.1)

The first web address to read is an exhaustive review of Snow Leopard is....

http://www.macintouch.com/specialreports/snowleopard/

The website to check for software compatibility is....

http://www.macintouch.com/specialreports/snowleopard/slcompat.html

A basic FAQ is also found at this site...

http://www.macintouch.com/specialreports/snowleopard/slfaq.html

I will sum up the highlights of what I think most users need to know about Snow Leopard. The first question to ask is "Can I install Snow Leopard on my Mac?

There are three requirements.

• **A Mac running an Intel Processor.** (go to the Apple Menu and choose About this Mac – it will say Intel in the processor line.

• **1 GB of Memory.** (again – go to the Apple Menu and choose About this Mac)

• **5 GB of free hard drive disk space.** (select your primary hard drive icon (Macintosh HD is the default) and go to the **File Menu** and select **Get Info**. There is an **Available** line.)

New OS Install Process for Snow Leopard

OK. You just checked and you can install Snow Leopard. Place the DVD inside the CD-

ROM drive, double-click on the DVD icon and then double-click on

the Install Mac OS X icon.

Notice: I did not say to Restart you Mac and hold down the "C" Key. The installer first runs in the Finder and copies needed files to the hard drive. It then reboots and completes the process. The install options for older OSes no longer exist.

You are then taken to the first OS X Install screen. The bottom is shown below.

Utilities... – Snow Leopard is different from other OS X installers. If you do a regular install, the process begins WITHOUT restarting your Mac. If you need to access Time Machine to back-up your Mac or Disk Utility, choose this option. The Mac will then ask you to Restart. This screen is shown on the next page.

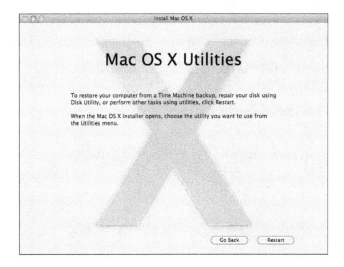

Continue – Click on this to begin the Install process if you are not using a Utility.

Customize... - This is where you decide what options you want to install with the Snow Leopard install. This screen is show below. I already installed Snow Leopard – so some options are missing below. I forgot about the manual before I installed.

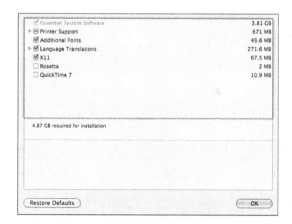

X11 – not require for most users. Can be un-checked.

Rosetta – This is software that will allow you make to run PowerPC software. You may need this for older applications. If you do not install it – Snow Leopard will allow you to install it after when it is needed.

QuickTime 7 - Snow Leopard install QuickTime X. It is discussed later in this manual. QuickTime 7 has more features and will install automatically if you purchased a QuickTime Pro license.

Printer Support – You can open this option as install only the printer drivers that you need. Canon or HP printers for example.

Language Translations – OS X is used around the world. You, however, do not need to have all of the languages around the world installed on your Mac. Un-check this box so that all these un-needed code is not installed.

Additional Fonts – Leave this as is – more fonts the merrier I say.

Clik on **OK** and then click on **Install** to begin the Install process. This should take about an hour to run.

Hard Drive Space – Snow Leopard does a lot of cleaning "under the hood." You should see several GBs more of free space after it is installed.

NOTE: Please run Verify Disk Permissions and Verify Disk using Disk Utility found in you Utilities folder or on you OS X 10.5 CD. It is better to start with a good hard drive than one that might have issues.

New Features

QuickTime X — This is the new version that ships with Snow Leopard. This version has is optimized for H.264 and AAC media formats. With the new inner-workings of Snow Leopard, this version is ready for what the future might bring. With this however, (at least for now) certain features available in QuickTime 7 are absent. You can now easily export to iTunes, YouTube or your MobileMe gallery (if you purchased this service from Apple). Trimming a video is the only edit function in the version so far. You can now take screen captures (as movies). You can also use your iSight camera for video as well.

How does it look????

Note that there is no border. The controls "float" in the window. From left to right on the bottom – the Controls. **Volume** (lower to higher), **Double arrow pointing to the left** – move the movie backwards in time, **Large Triangle pointing to right** – Play or Pause, **Double arrow pointing to the right** – move the movie forward in time, the **small box with**

an arrow coming out of it – this is gives you the export feature (iTunes, MobileMe and YouTube), **two arrows pointing in towards each other** – toggles between current size and full screen. It is hard to see in the example above, but the **lower right-hand corner** must be pressed and moved to scale the movie to the size you wish. I think you would agree that this feature is a little difficult to find on dark movies.

Once you push play – **ALL** of the controls disappear. Move the mouse to bring up the features again.

Recording – Below is the File Menu of the QuickTime X player. Note that here you can create new Audio, Screen or Movie recordings.

New Movie Recording	⌥⌘N
New Audio Recording	⌃⌥⌘N
New Screen Recording	⌃⌘N
Open File...	⌘O
Open URL...	⌘U
Open Recent	▶
Close	⌘W
Save As...	⇧⌘S
Save for Web...	⇧⌘E
Revert to Saved	

Save As... - Here you can save the movie in several formats. This window is shown on the next page.

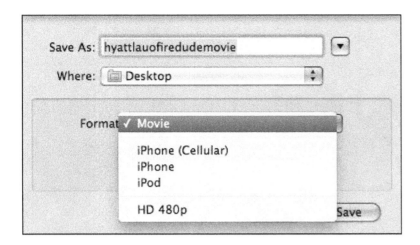

Save for web... - Export is optimized for the web. Screen shown below.

Put Back – Or the "woops" command. This command will take a file that was placed in the trash and return it back to where it was originally stored. This is found in the File Menu or right-clicking on the file in the trash. I am sure you will find this very useful. No more woops!!!

Location Services – Only used so far in the Date and Time System Preference, this is helpful for users who travel. An example is shown on the next page.

Energy Saver – This is really nice. While you Mac is sleeping and dreaming of more memory – the Mac is able to be woken up by an external device such as a Time Capsule device because of required network traffic. This is also useful for the Back to Mac feature of MobileMe. This System Preference is shown below – check off **Wake for network access**.

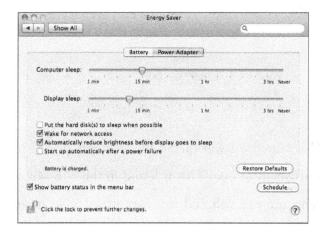

Services – This feature was not the greatest in earlier OSes. Now, when you access Services in Finder Menu – the Services that only apply to that file or folder are shown. This is shown below

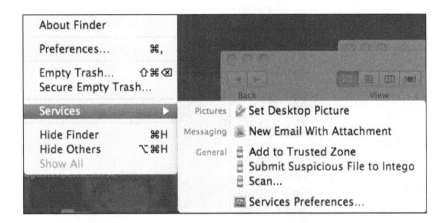

Expose  – This has a few enhancements. The first is that when you invoke Expose – the minimized documents in the dock appear as well. These are separated by a thin line. The windows are also aligned better. This is shown below.

Expose is now invoked when you click on an application icon in the dock. This is shown below.

Trackpad - Apple introduced certain keystroke commands that until now were only available to those laptops. With the advent of Snow Leopard – these items are now available to all laptops that support Snow Leopard. These features are show below. Trackpad is a System Preference.

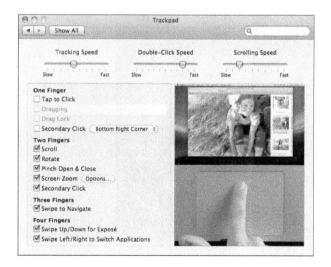

Mail – Now supports Microsoft Exchange Server. This also includes integration with Address Book and iCal.

Software that is known not to work – Snow Leopard is smarter when is comes to knowing what is broken (right now) and what works with it. After it is installed, Snow Leopard will place incompatible software into a folder called " Incompatible Software." This does not mean it will never work. Check the software list I mentioned above in this section or go to one of the Software Update sites mentioned in my useful website section.

AppleTalk – This network technology has been removed in this version of the OS. This primarily affects AppleTalk connected printers.

Column View – Is now sort able.

Text Substitution - If you go to the Language & Text System Preference – you can invoke auto substitute as you type.

Time Machine – Is now faster and its messages are more descriptive.

Stacks – You can now deeper into folders and back out again. You can now also sort Stacks as well.

The 64-bit question.

Much has been said about Snow Leopard being 64-bit. Older versions of the OS also had 64-bit parts as well. In Snow Leopard, the vast majority has been written to be 64-bit. This means that on Macs that support 64-bit, you should see a small speed increase. Not all Intel Macs support 64-bit. For Macs that support it – the default startup is still 32-bit. On some Macs, you can boot up in total 64-bit by pressing the 6 and 4 keys during startup. So, if you have hardware that supports it – you will see a speed increase. Unfortunately, as I said, not all Intel Macs can run 64-bit code. In the future as developers update their programs to support this feature – speed increases should be greater. You can also install huge amounts of RAM with a 64-bit Mac, but there is a realistic limit as to what you can and want to install.

OpenCL

OpenCL is a new way of accessing the much faster processors inside your Mac that handle graphics. With this technology and as software is updated to take use of it, the main CPU hands off tasks to the graphics cards or GPUs. Right now, only certain newer cards from NVIDIA and ATI are supported.

Grand Central Dispatch

Macintosh desktops and laptops contain multiple (processor) cores. Grand Central Dispatch is a new way to help speed up traffic between these cores. This done in a more efficient way and more importantly makes developers have an easier framework to take advantage of this technology. But, this is really new and it might take developers awhile to take full advantage of this.

10.6 conclusion

Snow Leopard re-wrote code that needed to updated or deleted code that was no longer needed. I have used it for awhile now and it is faster than Leopard (10.5). As developers rewrite their software to harness the new technologies within, the speed increase should grow. Snow Leopard is a system OS for the future. "Under the hood" improvements with a few new features. I attempted to write what I felt was necessary to know about this new OS. My 10.5 manual covers everything else that DID NOT change with Snow Leopard.

Final Thoughts....

I have been assisting Macintosh Users for many years. I enjoy helping them out whenever possible and guide them through their issues. I hope that this short guide has enlightened you in the ways of the Macintosh. I feel it covered what any new user should know about their newly purchased or going to be purchased Mac. The quick start guide missing from box of your new Mac. My other guides go into detail - the consumer software side of Apple – iWork and iLife. If you found this guide easy to use – I am sure you find these other two just as helpful.

Now stop reading this boring guide and go have fun on your Mac!!! I insist.

- Glen Durdik

Legal Information

© Glen Durdik 2010

iLife

iPhoto

iPhoto is a great way to organize your photos (and videos). You can edit photos, create personal cards, calendars or share one or all of them on the web. As with the other applications, I am going to go over all of the icons that appear on the window and all of the iPhoto menus. A sample of an iPhoto window – showing an event is shown below.

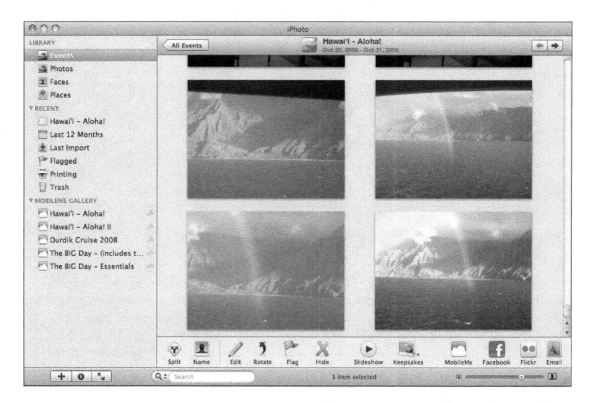

Note: I shrunk the screen so Keepsakes expanded is actually...

If you are launching iPhoto for the first time, there are a few screens you need to go through

to get to the main program. The first dialog box asks if you want to play a welcome video, view video tutorials or how to get hands-on training. This window is shown to the right. If you do not

need any of these items at this point, you can just click on the close button to start having photo fun in iPhoto.

The next is setting up locations in iPhoto. This dialog box is shown below.

The next item is very important. You are asked if you want iPhoto to run automatically

when you attach a camera. If you plan to use iPhoto for your entire photo needs – then say Yes and have it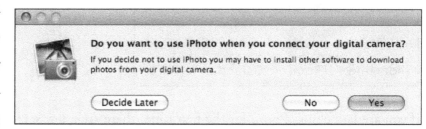

automatically run. The one downside is that it takes time to download the items into the program if you have a lot of items. If you select No, you can use a card reader and sort out the photos first before importing them into iPhoto. This window is shown above.

Breakdown of iPhoto Main Window

Library - Events

You can sort your photos into events. This makes it easier to create special personal projects or share them later. In the example above – I have two events – Hawai'i – Aloha! and Hawai'i Aloha II.

Library – Photos

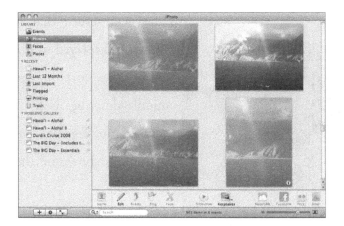

This just views all your photos in one big group. It is recommended to sort them out and create an event with the new photos you added.

Library – Faces

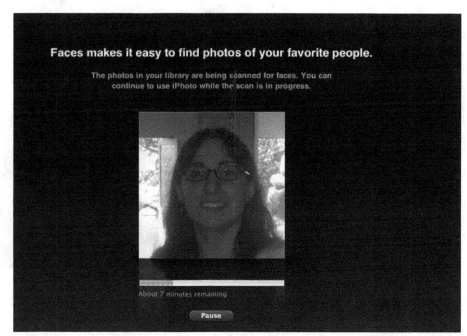

This is a way cool tool introduced in the latest version of iPhoto. The application is trained to pick out faces and have the ability to find them elsewhere in your Library. The first step is for iPhoto to run a short setup routine. This is shown to above.

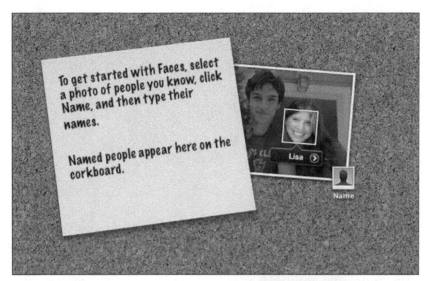

The next screen that is shown is displayed to the left. The note in the middle describes how to activate this feature. An example is shown on the next page.

Next, highlight the photo with the face you want to use and click on the **Name button**

. This brings up the screen on the right. Notice how it highlighted her face and gives you the option to name the person.

After this is done and go to Faces – you will see a picture of the face you named on a corkboard. If you select that person – all (hopefully) of the pictures with that name and face will show up. This is shown below.

Library – Places

Places allows you to give your photo geographic info. You can then view the area as "terrain" or a satellite view. Interesting – No? Here is an example…

1. Chose a picture from you album.
2. Click on the "I" button on the bottom right of the photo.
3. This brings up the following screen…

Click on photo place and highlight – Find on map…

This brings up the screen below. Type in the location (Island, State in this example)

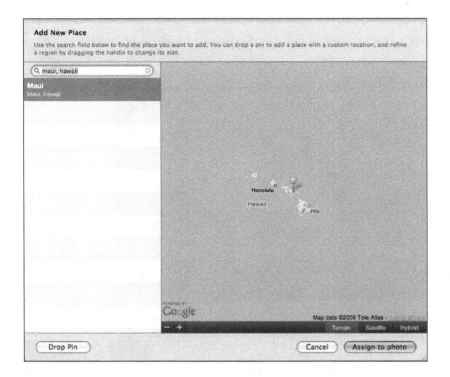

Click on **Assign to photo**. Finished. So – why is this useful? If you have zillions of pictures from family vacations – you can now see on a world map where you been. And once you pick a place on the map – you see all the photos from the location. Example below.

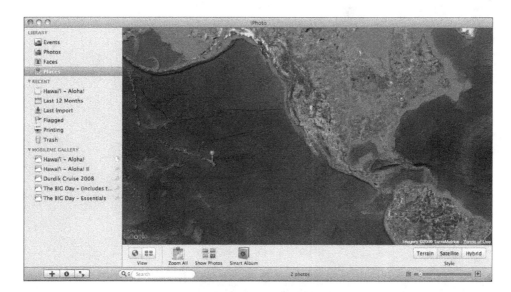

Notice that it is now on Satellite mode and I have been to Hawaii and New York. If I click and hold down the mouse on the pin in New York, it will show all the photos from New York (that I tagged as NY of course).

Recent

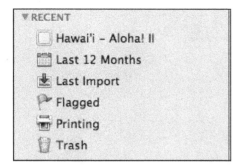

Simply, this brings up where you have been last, printed last or what is in the trash.

MobileMe

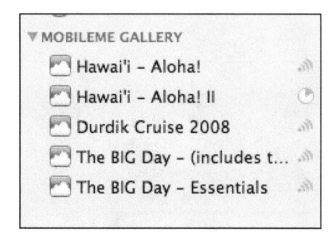

MobileMe allows you to quickly and easily share photos and videos on the web. In the example above, there are five events that I am sharing on web at the moment.

On the bottom right hand corner are two buttons that relate to **MobileMe**. It looks like this

. **Tell a Friend** just allows you to announce that a new gallery is being shared and gives the link to the new gallery in the email it generates.

Settings – Allows you to change how the gallery interacts with the viewers. This screen is shown below.

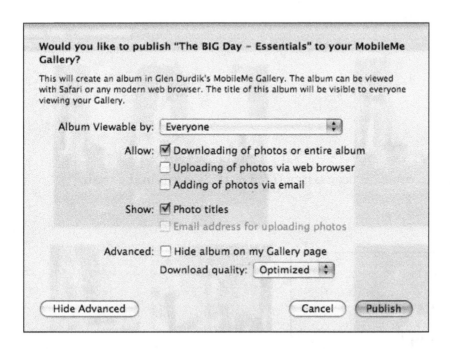

 This button allows you to create various new items in iPhoto. If you click this button – the screen below is brought up.

Note: See where it states Use selected items in new album. Use the select all command to grab all the photos in window. Hold down the **COMMAND** key while clicking on individual photos to take just the ones you want in the new album (book, card, calendar, slideshow).

 This button brings up basic info on a photo. A sample is shown on the next page.

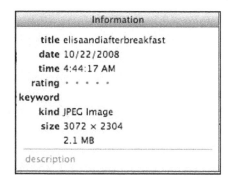

 This is the **Full Screen button**. Click on it and the photo takes up the whole screen. To get out of it – press the esc key.

 This is the **Search** tool. If the photos are named, you can search for items this way.

Name: Sets a name of a face in the photo

Notice that it thinks it is Elisa based on steps taken earlier. Click on the check mark to confirm.

Edit: Allows you to manipulate your photo in a variety of ways. These items are shown below. **Rotate** – rotates image 90 degrees every click. Crop – Highlight an area you want to keep and it removes the rest. Straighten – Free rotate the photo to make objects appear "more straight." **Enhance** – iPhoto evaluates your photo and tries to make it look the best it can be. Sometimes great. Sometimes not. Red-Eye – removes the red dots in the eyes of people in a photo due to a flash. Retouch – tried to remove blemishes from your photo.

Effects – See sample below

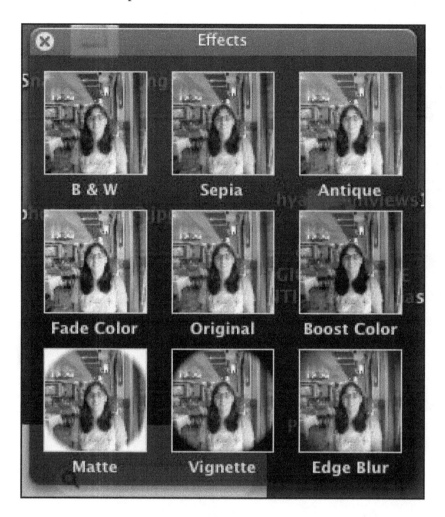

Adjust: For the more advanced user – which you should be in no time!

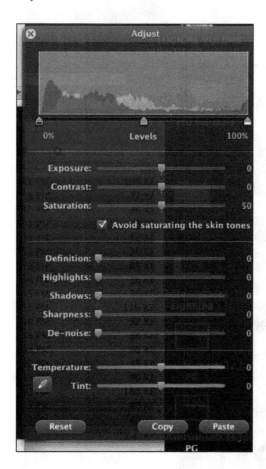

Slideshow: Allows you play a slideshow (automatically displays all selected photos at specific intervals.) If you move your mouse around the bottom middle of the screen, you are given the opportunity to modify the slideshow settings. A black and white toolbar will appear. On the left, you can click the left arrow to go back or the right arrow to move forward. If you click on one of the three icons next to the arrows, you change the theme, music and other settings.

Book: Want to create the ultimate coffee table book featuring your family? The Book feature allows you to create a professional quality book from the photos you chose. Notice the **Options and Prices button**. This book is created by Apple and this link explains all the details by going to an Apple website.

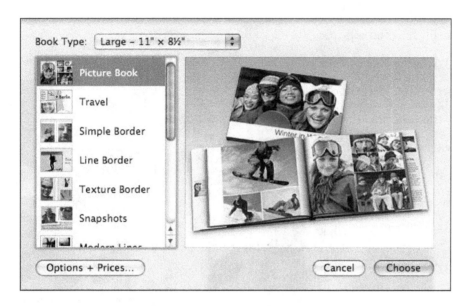

Here is a sample window of what steps are involved in creating book. This is a picture of the cover. You can choose themes, backgrounds, different layouts, etc. When you are done – click on **Buy Book.**

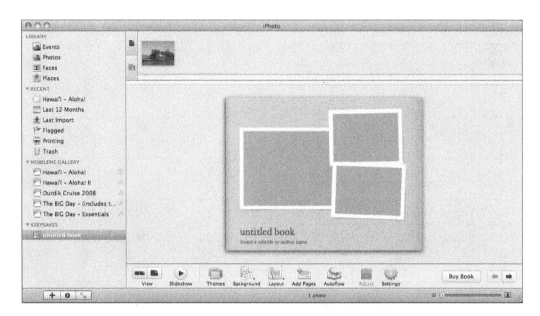

Calendar:

Create custom calendars in no time. So now there is no time like the present and make a calendar that has some meaning to you and your family.

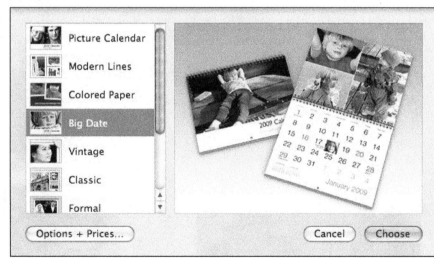

Here are some cool notes....

As you see in the example below – you can import iCal calendar events and birthdays (if present) from the Address book.

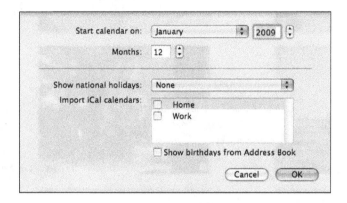

Card: Create your own special sentimental card with your photos here. I have selected Holiday/Events in the example to the right.

 Want the world to see your creative side? This buttons allow you to share your photos four different ways.

MobileMe: Below are all the options available to you when you publish your photos via **MobileMe.**

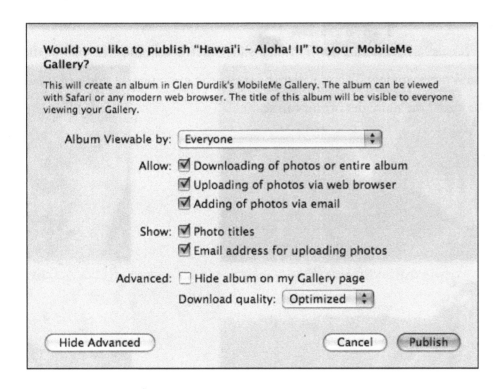

Facebook and **Flickr** are services that allow people to view your personally created websites describing yourself.

Mail: Allows you to send photos via email. Notice in the middle of sample below that you can specify the size of the photo (shrink it down to make it send/retrieved faster.

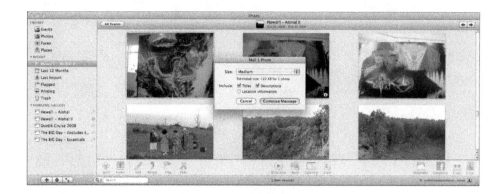

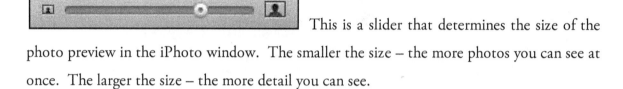This is a slider that determines the size of the photo preview in the iPhoto window. The smaller the size – the more photos you can see at once. The larger the size – the more detail you can see.

iPhoto Menus

iPhoto – iPhoto Menu

This menu has a few important items. **About iPhoto** tells you what version you have installed. **Preferences...** are discussed in detail next. You can **Empty the iPhoto trash** here or shop for iPhoto products. Last, you can **check for software updates via the Check for Updates... option**.

iPhoto – iPhoto Menu – Preferences – General

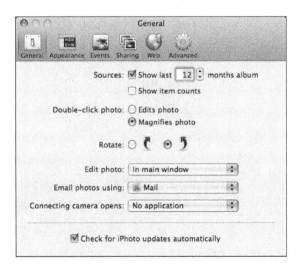

Sources – decide how many months you want to show and decide if you want to show item counts.

Decide whether or not a double-click on a photo edits or magnifies the photo. Decide what direction you want the default rotate to be. You can decide where to edit the photo – Main Window, Full Screen or a separate application all-together. You decide how you want to email photos. Last, decide if you want iPhoto, Image Capture or no application to be launched when a camera is connected. Oh, you can have iPhoto to automatically check for updates as well.

iPhoto – iPhoto Menu – Preferences – Appearance

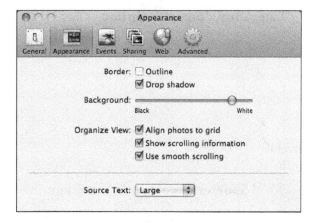

Border - decides whether you want a drop shadow or outline around your photos. **Background** – a slider that sets the color behind you pictures – it goes from all black to all white.

Organize View – the default is to have all three options checked. They are – Align photos to grid, show scrolling info and use smooth scrolling. The last option is to set source text as small or large.

iPhoto – iPhoto Menu – Preferences – Events

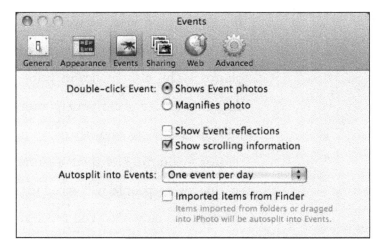

Double-click Event – can be set to either show event photos or magnify photos. **Show event reflections** – adds a reflection of the first event photo on your screen. You can also have iPhoto show scrolling information. **Autosplit into Events** – it can be one event per day, one event per week, two hour gap or an eight hour gap. Last, you check off the box to have items imported from the Finder autosplit.

iPhoto – iPhoto Menu – Preferences – Sharing

If you are on a local network, you can have iPhoto search for shared photos. This also applies to you – do you want to share your photos (all or part)? If you share your photos – you can give them a name so that other people will recognize them on the network. You can also give it a password as well.

iPhoto – iPhoto Menu – Preferences – Web

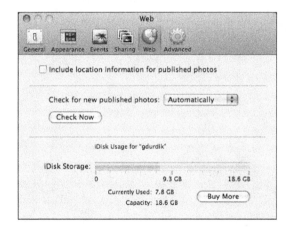

If you added location data to your photos – you can add this to your shared photos. You can check if there are any new published photos. Last, the window shows your iDisk usage and how much space you used and have left. Notice that you have the option to buy more space here as well.

iPhoto – iPhoto Menu – Preferences – Advanced

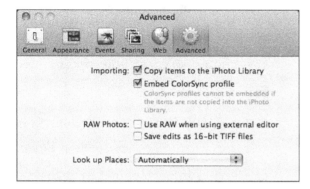

Importing – decide if you want new photos to be added to the iPhoto Library. It is on by default and most users will leave it on. You have the option to embed the ColorSync profile. ColorSync is a technology used by Apple that insures that colors are the same across Macs. There are other standards as well. **RAW Photos** – high-end cameras allow you to take these kinds of photos. These photos are better suited for image processing. **Look up Places** can be done automatically or never.

iPhoto – File Menu

New Album...	⌘N
New Album From Selection...	⇧⌘N
New Smart Album...	⌥⌘N
New Folder	⌥⇧⌘N
Get Info	⌘I
Import to Library...	⇧⌘I
Export...	⇧⌘E
Close Window	⌘W
Edit Smart Album	
Subscribe to Photo Feed...	⌘U
Order Prints...	
Print...	⌘P
Browse Backups...	

New Album – creates a new Album for you. **New Album from Selection** – if you want to create an album from a selected few photos – chose this option. **New Smart Album** – This will create an album based on criteria you set. It could be date, filename, face, place, etc. **New Folder** – creates and empty album. **Get Info** – gives you details on various characteristics of your photo. **Import to Library...** You can use this to take files not already in iPhoto and add them. (You can drag it in as well) **Export** – You can export your photo to a number of formats. These include – JPEG, TIFF, PNG, a web page, QuickTime Movie or slideshow. A slideshow, by default is sent to iTunes. You can subscribe to a photo feed. This is one place to go to if you want to order prints of your photos. **Browse Backups...** brings up Time Machine. If you accidentally or you child accidentally deleted a great photo – go here to get it back.

iPhoto – Edit Menu

Undo Rotate Photo	⌘Z
Redo	⇧⌘Z
Cut	⌘X
Copy	⌘C
Paste	⌘V
Select All	⌘A
Select None	⇧⌘A
Find	⌘F
Font	▶
Spelling	▶
Special Characters...	

Here you can "**undo**" an action or redo it if you decide to keep the change you made. **Cut** – Deletes what is highlighted. **Copy** – Puts what is highlighted into the Mac's clipboard. **Paste** – Takes what is in the clipboard and puts it into the area you are working on. **Select All** – Highlights all items at once. **Find** – Search iPhoto for a specific item. **Font** – Changes the font you are using. **Spelling** – checks the spelling of the text you have typed. **Special Characters** – gives you access to a window that shows all of the special characters found in each font.

iPhoto – Photo Menu

Show Extended Photo Info	⌥⌘I
Adjust Date and Time...	
Batch Change...	⇧⌘B
Rotate Clockwise	⌥⌘R
Rotate Counter Clockwise	⌘R
My Rating	▶
Flag Photo	⌘.
Hide Photo	⌘L
Duplicate	⌘D
Delete From Album	⌘⌫
Revert to Original	

Show Extended Photo Info – If you are a professional photographer – this item can be very useful as it gives a ton of info on the selected photo. **Adjust Date and Time...** - changes the date and time of the selected photo. **Rotate Clockwise or Counter Clockwise** – does what it says. **My rating** – you can assign ratings for each photo if you wish. **Flag Photo** – tags the photo with a flag and places it in the Flagged photo library as well. **Hide Photo** – Hides the photo from the window. You can go to the View Menu and select Hidden Photos to see them again. **Duplicate** –copied the entire photo and adds the copy to the album. **Delete from album** – deletes the photo from an album. **Revert to original** – Removes all changes done to photo.

iPhoto – Event Menu

Create Event
Create Event From Flagged Photos
Split Event
Make Key Photo
Add Flagged Photos To Selected Event
Open in Separate Window

Autosplit Selected Events

This menu creates events – empty or from flagged photos. **Split Event** – can split an event into smaller sections.   **Make Key Photo** – every event has a photo that shows up as the primary photo for the event – the photo you see in the Events Library. **Add Flagged Photos to Selected Event** – moves photos you flagged into an event of your choice.

Open in Separate Window – takes the event and put the photos in a new window – photos cannot be modified. **Autosplit Selected Events** – you can specify what day or time folder you want your imported photos to go into.

iPhoto - Share Menu

Email
Set Desktop

MobileMe Gallery
Facebook
Flickr

Send to iWeb ▶
Send to iDVD
Burn

This menu allows you to share you photos to the outside world through email, **Facebook**, **Flickr** or via a **MobileMe** gallery. You can set you desktop to be the picture of you choice here as well. You can send it iWeb or iDVD. Last, you can burn the images onto a CD-R.

iPhoto – View Menu

Titles	⇧⌘T
Rating	⇧⌘R
Keywords	⇧⌘K
Event Titles	⇧⌘F
Hidden Photos	⇧⌘H
Sort Photos	▶
Show in Toolbar	▶
Full Screen	⌥⌘F
Always Show Toolbar	
Thumbnails	▶

This menu allows you to decide what info is displayed with your photo. It allows you to see hidden photos. **Show in Toolbar** – gives you the choice to add other items besides the default ones. Set desktop and printing are two choices.

iPhoto – Window Menu

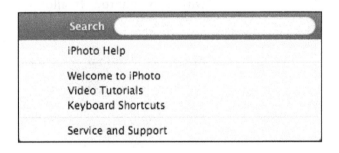

Minimize – shrinks the iPhoto window and places it in the dock. To get it back – click on the icon in the dock. **Zoom** – makes the window the largest it can be. **Manage My Places** – If you place location data into the info section of a photo – you can modify the locations here. **Bring All to Front** – If you have many applications open – you can bring all iPhoto windows to the top of the stack of open windows.

iPhoto – Help Menu

This is the place to go to when you ask, "How do I do that??" My manual is a good primer for users – but this menu covers a lot of items in more detail.

What's New in iPhoto '11?

There are several amazing new additions and changes to iPhoto. In this section, I will go over what they are and how each works. But first...above is the new Welcome Screen when you first launch iPhoto. **Note: allows backup your hard drive before upgrading any software package. Apple released an update that should avoid an upgrade problem that affects your iPhoto Library and application.**

After you Click on Close...you get the following screen....

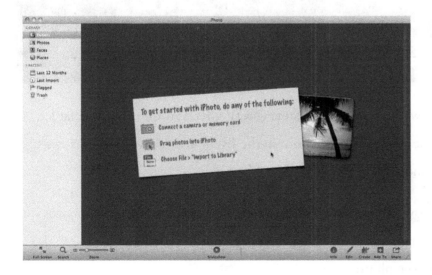

Full Screen Mode:

This allows you to see you photo on the screen with minimal distractions – no Mac Desktop…just the photo and the options to modify it. The button to activate this feature is located on the bottom left of you iPhoto window. An example of Full Screen is shown below.

On the top of the window, we have the Event name (NOV CRUISE ONE) on the far left. On the far right, we have the number of the photo in the Event and left and right arrows to go to the previous or next photo.

On the bottom of the window, we have the Full Screen icon, a visual guide of the photos prior and after the one you are currently looking at the far right of the screen, and several options you can perform on the photo.

Info: This gives you specifics on photo itself. In the example below, it shows it was taken by a Canon PowerShot G11, the size of the photo and the type of image (JPEG).

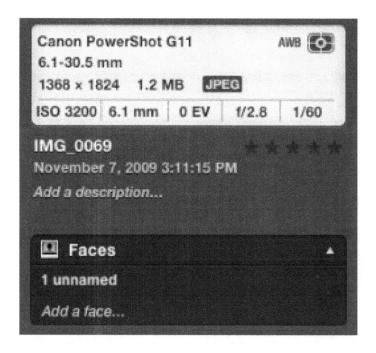

Edit: This gives you access to the three menus of changes available for your photo. Below are **Quick Fixes.**

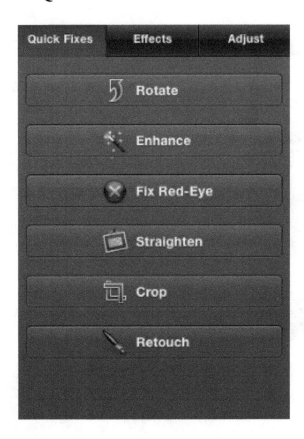

Rotate: Rotates your photo 90 degrees at a time.

Enhance: Does some magical work to your picture to try and fix it so that looks as its best. You can undo it if you don't like its effect.

Fix Red –Eye: If you used a flash, the subject in your photo might have red eyes. This attempts to remove the redness.

Straighten: Allows you to fix the alignment of your photo. This option is shown below.

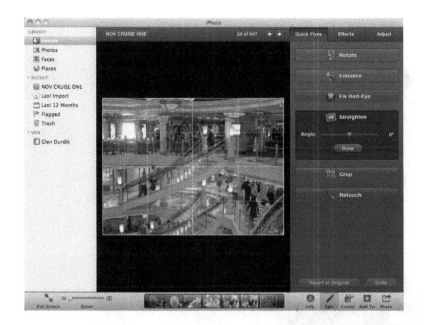

Crop: Allows you to cut out unwanted parts of your photo. This is shown below.

Retouch: This allows you to remove blemishes in a photo. This is shown below.

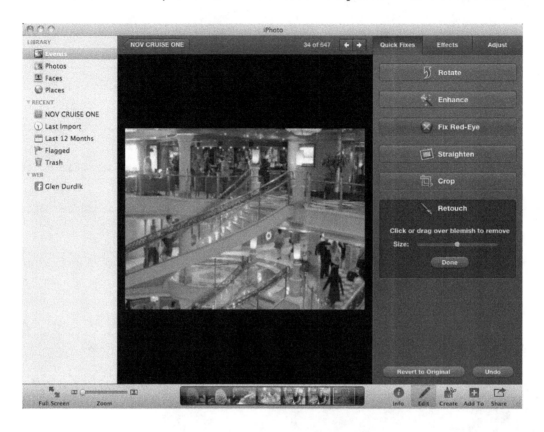

Effects: You have different choices than the older version of iPhoto. The options now available are shown below.

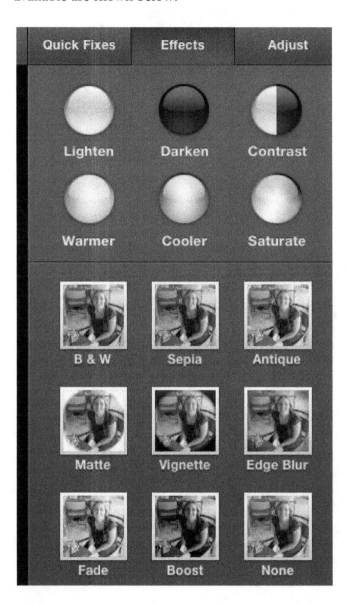

Adjust Setting is the same in both versions.

Create: This is found next to Edit. It allows you to create a new Album, book or Card from the photos you have selected. This is shown to the right. **Note: Calendars are restored after you apply the 9.1 update.**

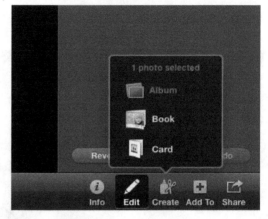

Creating a Book:

The first screen that appears in shown above. You can chose from a variety of themes and choose either a Hardcover, Softcover or Wire-bound type of book. Click on Create to start the process. After you are done, you can place an order with Apple for the awesome new project you just created!!!

Creating a Card:

This is similar to creating a book. You must choose a design and layout and customize the card to make it your own. You can choose between **Letterpress** (shown below), **Folded** or **Flat**.

Add to: This allows you to add the current photo you are working on to an Album, Slideshow, Book or Card. This is shown below.

Share: Here you can share you precious memories with the world!!! You can **order prints** from Apple, add to a **MobileMe Gallery** (a fee based service from Apple), **Flickr**, **Email** and updated support for **Facebook**. I will cover changes to Facebook and Email starting on the next page.

Facebook – First, you have to log into Facebook to add items. This is shown below.

Next, choose where you want it to go…. Profile Picture, New Album or add to an existing Album.

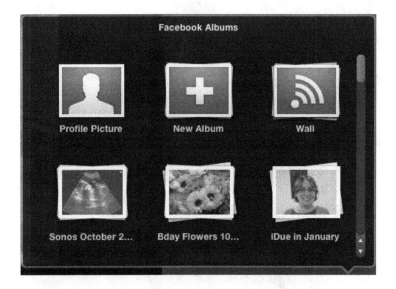

One new feature is having comments made on the photos uploaded to Facebook now appear in iPhoto as well.

Email: iPhoto has exciting new ways to share your memories via email. You can chose between eight different templates. You choose them for the different icons on the right hand side of your screen. On the bottom of this window, you can choose to attach the photos to the email or not. This window is shown below.

Here are examples of every template available....

Snapshots.

Corkboard.

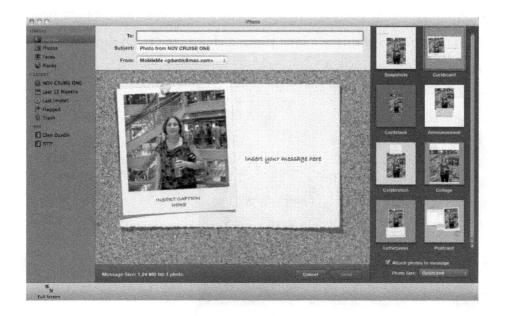

Cardstock.

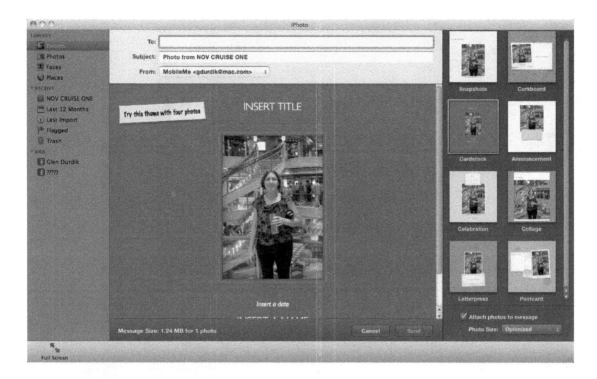

Announcement.

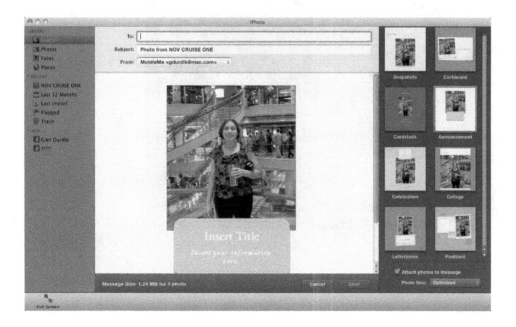

Celebration.

Letterpress.

Postcard.

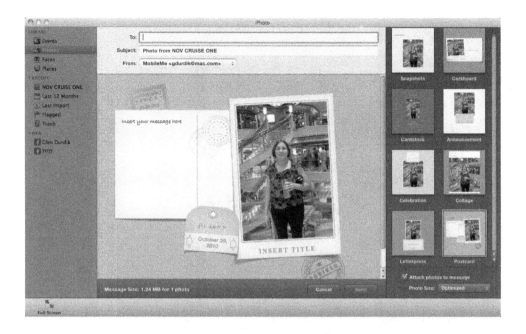

Slideshows: There are now 12 slideshow themes to choose from. They are shown below.

You can create a slideshow when you are viewing your photos. On the bottom of the

window - in the middle is the Slideshow button . Click on it to begin Presentation Nirvana.

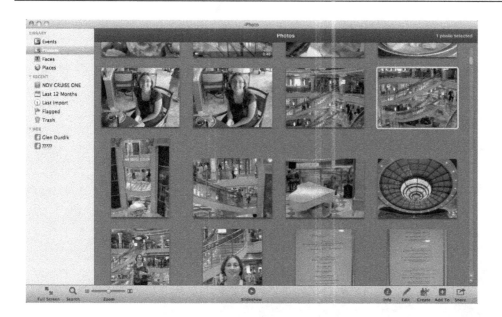

Once you selected your theme, you can start it or with the control bar shown below change other options. The left arrow goes to the previous picture, the parallel lines pause the slideshow, the right arrow brings you to the next picture, the Theme (slides graphic), the musical notes allows you to change the music and Setting (the gear) allows you to change a few other options. Music and Settings are show on the next page.

Music.

Music Source: You have the following for choices...

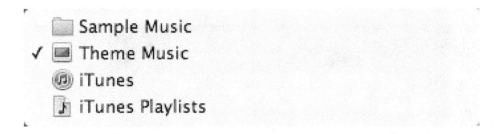

Settings.

Slideshow Themes: One example.

It is tough showing off powerful animation features in a written guide. I just wanted to show you one example – Mobile. This is shown below.

On the count of three...say Cheese!! Now you have a good background on how iPhoto works and all of the great things you can do with it. iPhoto is more powerful then ever...explore, have fun and create awesome projects!!!

iLife

iDVD

iDVD makes it very easy to create professional looking DVDs in a flash. If you have time to

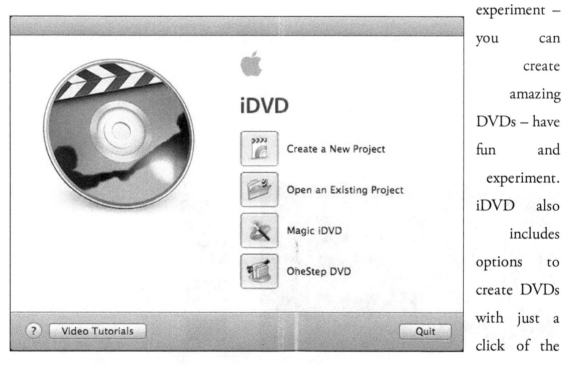

experiment – you can create amazing DVDs – have fun and experiment. iDVD also includes options to create DVDs with just a click of the mouse. To the left is the first screen you see when you launch iDVD. I will cover all the options here as well the toolbars and menus in the coming pages.

If you click on **Create a New Project** – the first options to come up are to name the project and decide if you want it to be widescreen (large rectangle as opposed to standard which is more square) or not. This is shown to the below.

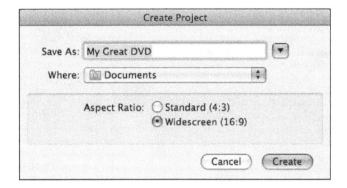

The next screen is the main workspace for iDVD. This is shown below.

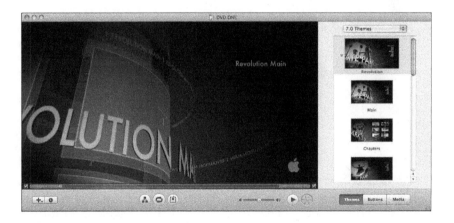

 This button adds a new Submenu, Movie or Slideshow to your project.

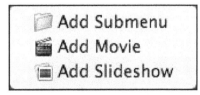

 This button gives you access to info on all aspects of your project. This includes Background, Audio, Buttons and Drop Zones.

This is called the DVD Map. It is a nice way to visualize your project. The main work area is the area to the left where there is a grey box and a blue box. You can add elements here – a most intuitive way to add items.

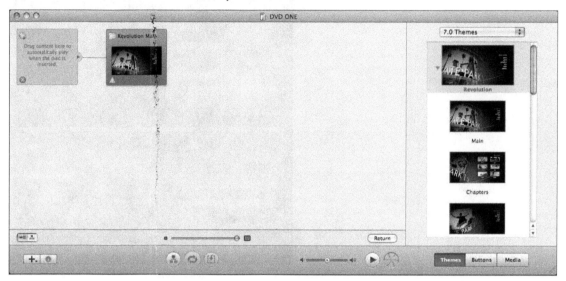

This button starts or stops motion.

This button allows you to edit drop zones. An example is shown to the right.

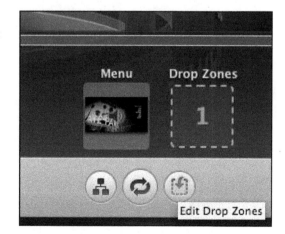

 This slider just controls the volume of playback.

 This button simulates a PLAY of your project.

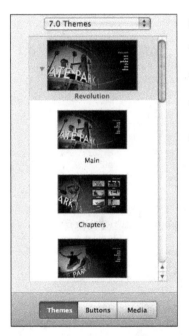 This button activates the BURN of your project to a DVD. Depending on the amount of media in your project – this could take quite sometime to complete.

On the far right of the screen – you will see three buttons. They are Themes, Buttons and Media. The first button – **Themes** is shown to the left. Notice that it states 7.0 themes. This is actually a drop down menu and gives you access to earlier themes as well.

The next is **Buttons**. This allows you to add one of the available icons to an added submenu for example.

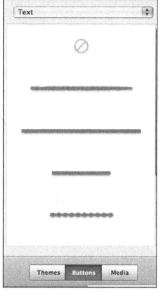

The last button is **Media**. This gives you access to all of your media files found in **iPhoto**, **iTunes** or an **iMovie** movie file.

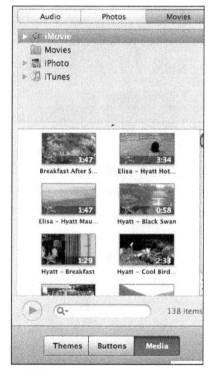

 This item found in the media window allows you to search files that meet your criteria.

iDVD – Menus

iDVD – iDVD Menu

About iDVD
Preferences...   ⌘,
Shop for iDVD Products
Provide iDVD Feedback
Register iDVD
Check for Updates...
Services   ▶
Hide iDVD   ⌘H
Hide Others   ⌥⌘H
Show All
Quit iDVD   ⌘Q

This contains a few important items. **About iDVD** – tells you what version you are running. **Check for Updates...** goes online to check to see if there are updates. **Preferences...** are discussed in detail below.

iDVD – iDVD Menu – Preferences – General

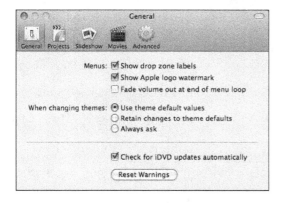

This menu window allows you to specify if menus show drop zone labels, decide if you want to show the Apple logo watermark or fade volume out at the end of a menu loop. If you change themes – you can specify it to use theme default values, retain changes to theme defaults or always ask. Here you can have iDVD always check for updates.

iDVD – iDVD Menu – Preferences – Projects

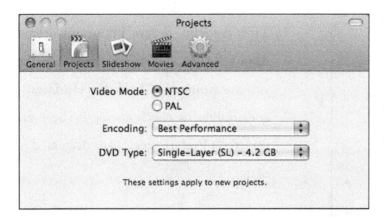

Video Mode: North America and Europe have different standards. NTSC is the default – which is North America. **Encoding** - you can chose between Best Performance, High Quality or Professional Quality. **DVD Type** – specifies what type of DVD you use – Single Layer (most common) or Double Layer

iDVD – iDVD Menu – Preferences – Slideshow

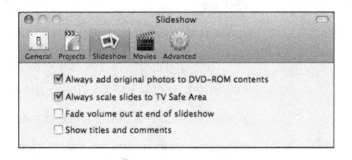

Here you have four options when creating slides. They are: decide if you always wan to add original photos to DVD-ROM contents (should leave on), always scale slides to TV Safe Area, fade volume put at the end of a slideshow and if you want to show titles and comments.

iDVD – iDVD Menu – Preferences – Movies

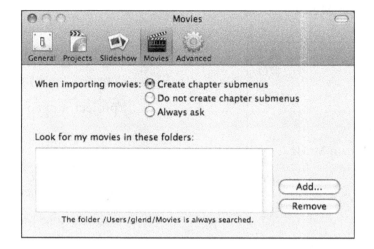

There are two basic questions asked here. One – when you import a movie – do you want it to create a chapter submenu or not. Second – where do you want iDVD to look for movies.

iDVD – iDVD Menu – Preferences – Advanced

The first option is to set where your themes are located. The one in the window to the left is the default one. You can add others if you like. **OneStep** is discussed later. The **Preferred DVD Burning Speed** is set to Maximum possible by default. You can it to a slower speed if you prefer.

iDVD – File Menu

New...	⌘N
Open...	⌘O
Open Recent	▶
Magic iDVD...	
OneStep DVD	
OneStep DVD from Movie...	
Close Window	⌘W
Save	⌘S
Save As...	⇧⌘S
Archive Project...	
Save Theme as Favorite...	
Import	▶
Burn DVD...	⌘R
Save as Disc Image...	⇧⌘R
Save as VIDEO_TS folder...	

Here you can create a new project, open a save project or open a recently opened project. You can also **Save** or perform a **Save As...** here as well. You can **Burn a DVD** here, **Save it as a Disc Image** or **VIDEO_TS folder**.

iDVD – File Menu - Magic iDVD...

Magic iDVD takes out a lot of the planning out of making a new DVD. You enter a title, choose a theme, drag in movies and photos and instant DVD project file is created.

iDVD – File Menu – OneStep DVD

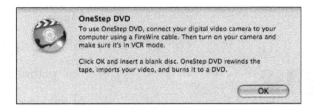

This option is very simple. Connect your video camera via Firewire. Turn it on and set it to VCR mode. Insert a blank DVD. Click on OK. Videotape to DVD in time flat. No bells and whistles, but fast.

iDVD – Edit Menu

Undo Add Movie	⌘Z
Redo	⇧⌘Z
Cut	⌘X
Copy	⌘C
Paste	⌘V
Paste and Match Style	⌥⇧⌘V
Delete	
Duplicate	⌘D
Copy Style	⌥⌘C
Paste Style	⌥⌘V
Select All Buttons	⌘A
Select None	⇧⌘A
Special Characters...	

Here you can **undo** or **redo** a recent change. You can **Cut** items out, **Copy** them or after copied, **Paste** them into your project somewhere else. You can **Delete** or **Duplicate** elements of you project. You can **Select All Buttons** if you wish. You also have access to **Special Characters...** as well. These are unique symbols or graphics not normally seen when you access a font.

iDVD - Project Menu

Project Info...	⇧⌘I
Switch to Standard (4:3)	⌥⌘A
Edit Drop Zones	
Autofill Drop Zones...	⇧⌘F
Add Submenu	⇧⌘N
Add Movie	⇧⌘O
Add Slideshow	⌘L
Add Text	⌘K
Add Title Menu Button	
New Menu from Selection	
Go Back	⌘B

Project Info... Shown on Next Page. You can switch your DVD back or forth form Standard to Widescreen. You can Edit Drop zones here. You can add a Submenu, Movie, Slideshow, Text or Title Menu Button.

iDVD - Project Menu – Project Info...

This gives you all the important data in regards to your project.

iDVD – View Menu

Motion	⌘J
Show Map	⇧⌘M
Show Inspector	⌘I
Hide Motion Playhead	
Show TV Safe Area	⌘T
Show Standard Crop Area	⌥⌘T

In this menu – you can determine what tools are to been seen on your screen.

iDVD – Advanced Menu

Apply Theme to Project
Apply Theme to Submenus
Reset Object to Theme Settings
✓ Loop movie
Create Chapter Markers for Movie
✓ Encode in Background
Delete Encoded Assets
Edit DVD–ROM Contents...

In this menu – you decide if you want to apply a theme to a Project or to Submenus. You can have it set to encode items in the background. You can also delete already encoded assets. Last, you can edit DVD-ROM Contents.

iDVD – Window Menu

Minimize	⌘M
Zoom	
Actual Size	⌘1
Fit to Screen	
Bring All to Front	

Here you can **Minimize** a window to the dock or **Zoom** the screen to its largest size. You can also set it the screen to its **Actual size** or **Fit to screen**. If you have a lot of programs open, you can bring all windows related to iDVD to the top by selecting – **Bring All to Front.**

iDVD – Help Menu

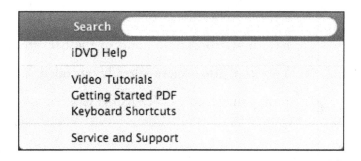

This menu allows you to search for help on items, access Video Tutorials, or the Getting Started PDF. You also have access to a list of keyboard shortcuts.

That's iDVD. Ready to become the next Hollywood Mogul? Have fun trying out new things and share you wonderful events with everyone.

iLife

iMovie

iMovie is a great program. It can be used with just a learning a few basic steps or it can involve a lot of complicated additions to help make a good movie a great movie. As with the other guides – I just want to go over the very basics of the program. Learn where everything is located via this manual. Sit down and explore for a few minutes or hours and learn to become a great video editor. That being said, let's begin… The first screen you encounter is the Welcome screen. As with the other applications – you have access to online tutorials or welcome video to help get you started. Click on the close button to begin creating the next blockbuster.

On the next page is the Main Screen of iMovie. It consists of three parts. They are the **Preview Window, Project Window and Event Window.** I used iMovie a few months ago to edit them and post them via **MobileMe** on the Internet.

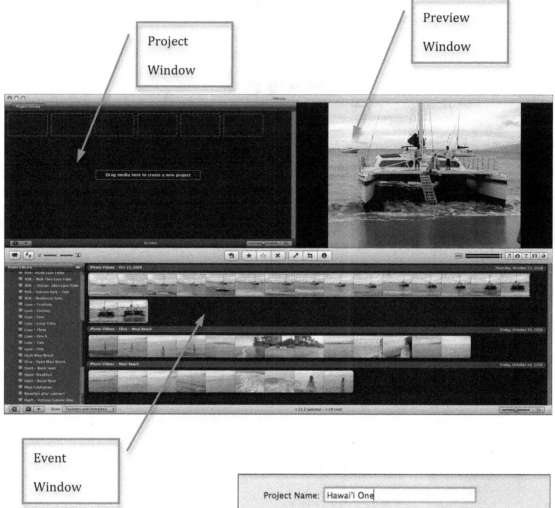

Notice in the example above, there is no project in the **Project Window**. If I drag an event from the **Event window** – I am asked to create a new Project. This is shown to the right. Here you must give it a name, decide if it is Widescreen or Standard and choose a Theme. You can have it also automatically add transitions and titles if you prefer.

Project Window Buttons

The button on the far left plays the video at full screen. The button next to it plays the video from the beginning.

This tells you the time of the video in the Project window. (I imported a short video after taking the screenshot of the main window above.)

iMovie shows a "picture" of moments in your video to show a preview of the entire video. In the example here – this picture occurs every 5 seconds until the end of the clip.

Below Project Window

Camera Import Button. If you have an iSight camera – this will pop up when

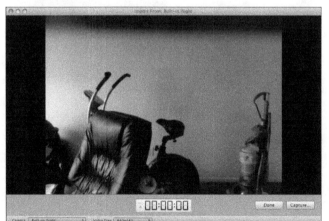

you click on it. If you attach a video camera this will show up as well. The sample window is shown to the left. Click on **Capture...** to begin recording. Click on **Done** to return to iMovie.

Swap Project Window with Event Window. In my example – Project is on top and Event is on the bottom. You can reverse the two if you prefer.

 This slider determines the size of the snapshot pictures of your clip(s) or complete movie.

 If you want to add a short highlighted clip to your project – highlight the frames and click on this button. This adds the selection to you project.

 The first star marks the highlighted clip as a Favorite. The second – hollow star "unmarks" the selection. The X button rejects the clip and deletes it from the complete clip.

This button allows you to add a Voiceover to your clip(s).

 If you just want a certain area of your clip to be on the screen – use this tool called Crop. You could just have a video cropped to show one face in a large crowd for example.

This is the **Inspector button**. It gives you a nice summary of the clip. This is shown to the right.

 This feature shows you the left and right volume of the sound in your clip(s).

 This button allows you to show the music and sound effects window. This is shown to the right. Note that is has access to your **iTunes Library, iLife Sound Effects and iMovie Sound Effects.**

This button brings up the **Photo browser**. This is shown aboce. Notice that it brings up iPhoto items.

This button brings up the **Title browser**. This is shown to the below.

This button brings up the **Transitions browser**. The options available are shown below. If you click on the title, you see a brief preview of the effect.

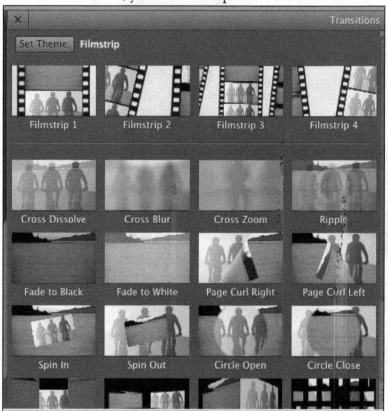

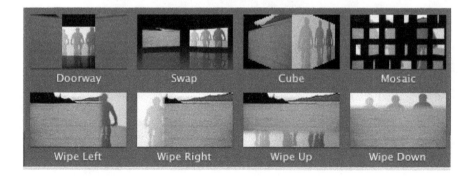

This button brings up the **Map and Background** browser. The options available are shown to the right.

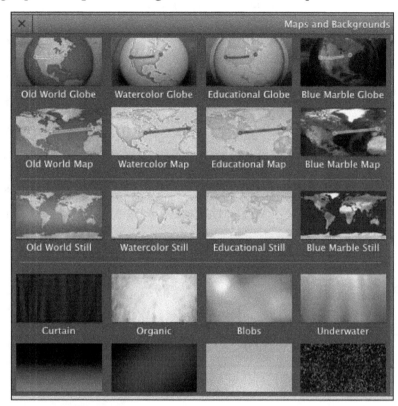

 This button deals with Events. In the example of the main window I used at the beginning of this guide - there is a list of events on the left and to the right of that – the actual clips with the snapshot pictures. If you click this button – the text part of the Event window will disappear and leave just the clips showing.

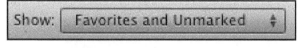 This also deals with Events. You have the choice of Favorites and Unmarked, Favorites only, All clips or Rejected ones.

iMovie Menus

iMovie – iMovie Menu

About iMovie	
Preferences...	⌘,
Shop for iMovie Products	
Provide iMovie Feedback	
Register iMovie	
Check for Updates...	
Hide iMovie	⌘H
Hide Others	⌥⌘H
Show All	
Quit iMovie	⌘Q

This menu contains a few important items. **About iMovie** - tells you what version you are running. You can further down – check for updates manually. **Preferences**... are discussed below.

iMovie – iMovie Menu – Preferences - General

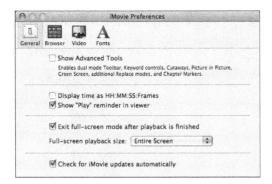

The first option asks if you want to show **Advanced Tools**. These include Cutaways, Picture in Picture, Green Screen and a few others. Not for the more casual user. You can display time as HH:MM:SS:Frames. You can have the "Play" reminder in viewer, set if you want to exit full-screen mode after playback is finished. You can set Full-screen to entire screen, double, actual or half. Last, you can set iMovie to check for updates automatically.

iMovie – iMovie Menu – Preferences - Browser

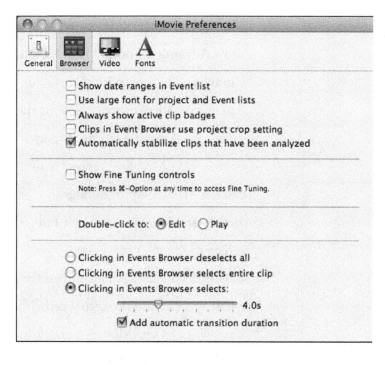

This menu is broken down into four sections. The first section on top allows you to show date ranges in the Event list, Use large font for project and Event lists, decide if you want to always show active clip badges, decide if you want clips in the Event browser to use project crop settings and last – automatically stabilize clips that have been analyzed. The second section asks if you want to show Fine Tuning controls. The third section asks what to do with a double-click – Edit or Play. The last section deals with mouse clicking on various items in iMovie.

iMovie – iMovie Menu – Preferences - Video

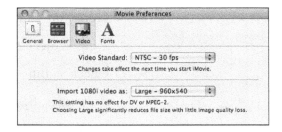

Video Standard – Can be NTSC or PAL. Every region has different standard. The U.S. uses NTSC. You can also set what happens when you import HD video – large or Full.

iMovie – iMovie Menu – Preferences - Fonts

This menu sets the color and Font combinations. You are not limited to the fonts shown to the left.

iMovie – File Menu

New Project...	⌘N
New Folder...	
New Event	
Duplicate Project	
Project Properties...	⌘J
Move Entire Clip to Trash	⌘⌫
Move Rejected Clips to Trash	
Space Saver...	
Consolidate Media...	
Merge Events...	
Split Event Before Selected Clip	
Adjust Clip Date and Time...	
Analyze for Stabilization	
Import from Camera...	⌘I
Import	▶
Page Setup...	⇧⌘P
Print Event...	⌘P

Here you can create a **New Project or Event**. Check out Project Properties. **Space Saver** moves rejected clips to the Trash.   You can also print an event if you wish.

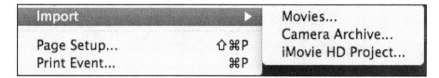

Import options found in the File Menu.

iMovie – Edit Menu

Undo Change Title	⌘Z
Redo	⇧⌘Z
Cut	⌘X
Copy	⌘C
Paste	⌘V
Paste Adjustments	▶
Reject Selection	⌫
Reject Entire Clip	⌥⌫
Select Entire Clip	⌘A
Select	▶
Trim to Selection	⌘B
Trim Clip End	▶
Split Clip	⇧⌘S
Join Clip	
Detach Audio	
Mute Clip	⇧⌘M
Reveal in Event Browser	
Arrange Music Tracks...	
Unpin Music Track	
Add Beat Marker	M
Spelling	▶
Special Characters...	⌥⌘T

As this program deals with adding or deleting items to achieve a final movie – there are a lot of options found in this menu.

iMovie - View Menu

```
Favorites Only
✓ Favorites and Unmarked          ⌘L
  All Clips
  Rejected Only

  Group Events By Disk
  Group Events By Month
✓ Most Recent Events at Top
  Show Separate Days in Events

  Play                           space
  Play Selection                     /
  Play from Beginning                \
  Play Around Current Frame          ▶
  Play full-screen                  ⌘G

✓ Snap to Ends
✓ Snap to Beats                    ⌘U
✓ Audio Skimming                   ⌘K
  Playhead Info                    ⌘Y
```

This menu allows you great control over how items are viewed. There are five options for Play for example.

iMovie – Text Menu

```
  Show Fonts          ⌘T

  Bold              ⇧⌘B
  Italic            ⇧⌘I
  Underline         ⇧⌘U
  Outline           ⇧⌘O

  Bigger             ⌘+
  Smaller            ⌘−

  Align               ▶
  Kern                ▶
  Ligature            ▶
  Baseline            ▶

  Copy Style        ⌥⌘C
  Paste Style       ⌥⌘V
```

This menu deals exclusively with fonts. It gives you control over changing various characteristics.

iMovie - Share Menu

```
iTunes...
iDVD
Media Browser...
YouTube...
MobileMe Gallery...

Export Movie...                    ⌘E
Export using QuickTime...
Export Final Cut XML...

Remove from iTunes
Remove from Media Browser...
Remove from MobileMe Gallery...
Remove from YouTube...
```

Show your work to the world! Here you can **send it to iTunes or iDVD**. Share it on the Internet via **YouTube** or **MobileMe**. **Final Cut** is a truly professional application far more advanced then iMovie.

iMovie – Window Menu

```
Minimize                          ⌘M
Minimize All
Zoom

Precision Editor                  ⌘/
Clip Trimmer                      ⌘R

Clip Adjustments                  I
Video Adjustments                 V
Audio Adjustments                 A
Cropping, Ken Burns & Rotation    C

Show Projects full-screen         ⌘6
Show Events full-screen           ⌘7

Show Project Library
Hide Event Library
Viewer                            ▶
Swap Events and Projects

Music and Sound Effects           ⌘1
Photos                            ⌘2
Titles                            ⌘3
Transitions                       ⌘4
Maps and Backgrounds              ⌘5
```

This menu gives you a ton of options as to what you want to see when editing a movie clip. Clip, Video, Audio adjustments or the Music and Sound effect browser, photo browser, etc.

iMovie – Help Menu

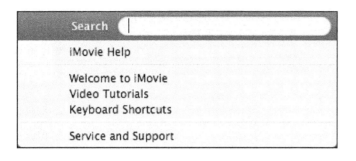

There is A LOT to learn to effectively use this program. Use this guide to get started. Access the features of this menu for further advice and guidance.

What's New in iMovie '11?

There are a lot of cool new features in iMovie. This includes creating Movie Trailers adding special effects like slow motion and instant replay, easy audio controls and new Sports and News themes.

Let me start with creating a movie trailer. The first step is to go to the File Menu and choose New Project. This will bring up the screen below.

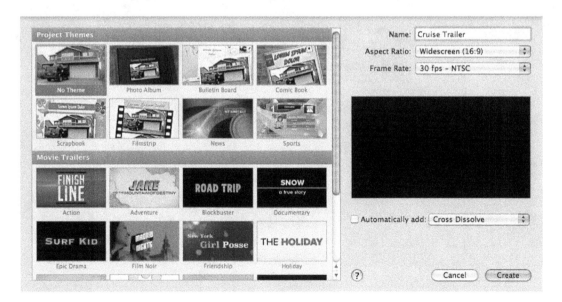

You are given the choice of 15 different trailers. They are **Action, Adventure, Blockbuster, Documentary, Epic Drama, Film Noir, Friendship, Holiday, Love Story, Pets, Romantic Comedy, Sports, Spy, Supernatural** and **Travel**. Choose the one you, give it a name in the upper right hand corner of the screen, determine it you want it to be widescreen or not and finally the frame rate. 30 fps (frames per second) NTSC is probably fine for most projects.

Next, fill in the **Outline** of you trailer.

You are given the choice of Logo Style under the Studio section. Below are the choices available.

> *Black Background*
> *Spinning Earth in Space*
> *Sun Rays Through Clouds*
> ✓ *Snowy Mountain Peak*
> *Glowing Pyramid*
> *Signals Across the Globe*

This is the bottom of the Outline Section. Also note – the preview window on the right, which shows the final result.

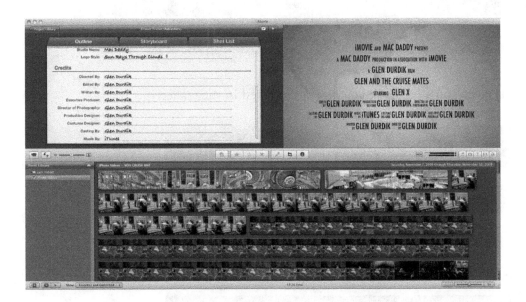

Storyboard: This is the next step in filling out the items needed for the trailer. Below is a sample with no media inserted.

Short List: This gives you a list of the media you inserted in the trailer.

That's it!!! It might take a while to find the short clips needed for every segment of the trailer, but it does come out great when you are done.

Sports and News Themes: You are given two new theme choices. These are shown below.

The Sports theme sounds terrific if you create videos for your sports teams or your child's sports team. You are given the option to create actual Team Rosters that can be used in the creation of a movie using the Sports theme. Below is an example of the **Sports Team Editor** that helps create the teams for you.

Analyze video for People: This is like Faces in iPhoto. You can have iMovie scan your existing movies in iMovie or scan during import for the presence of people. This can help you out later when you want to add "people" clips to your project. To perform this task during an import, select "**After import analyze for**" and choose either **Stabilization and People** or just **People**. To do this function to files already in your library, go to the **File**

Menu and select **Analyze Video** and then choose **People**. This could take awhile for long clips. Go get a coffee or watch TV for a bit. After this is done, you will see a People button appear below the Event browser. You can then click on the People button to see just the frames that include People in them.

Fast Forward, Slow Motion and Instant Replay: You can now add these effects to your work. They are found in the **Clip Menu**. This is shown below.

Options for **Fast Forward...**

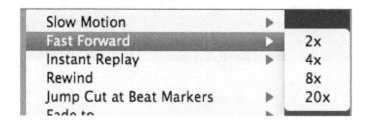

Options for **Slow Motion...**

Slow Motion	▶	50%
Fast Forward	▶	25%
Instant Replay	▶	10%
Rewind		

Options for **Instant Replay...**

Slow Motion	▶	
Fast Forward	▶	
Instant Replay	▶	50%
Rewind		25%
Jump Cut at Beat Markers	▶	10%
Fade to	▶	

Share Options – expanded. Besides the choices in the older version of iMovie, you can share it to **Vimeo, CNN iReport and Podcast Producer**. The new Share Menu is shown below.

Media Browser...
iTunes...
iDVD...

MobileMe Gallery...
YouTube...
Facebook...
Vimeo...
CNN iReport...
Podcast Producer...

Export Movie...   ⌘E
Export using QuickTime...
Export Final Cut XML...

Remove from   ▶

Animatics.

This is a new feature added to the Maps and Background window. It allows you to add "placeholders" for spots where you think you might add people to the video. The choices available are shown below.

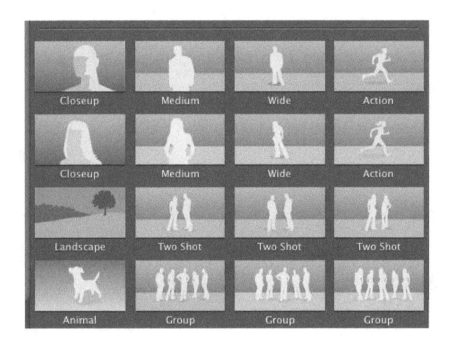

Remember me when you win you first Academy award!! I hope I helped explain this complex program in these few pages. Now you know where everything is located – start shooting video and make the next Blockbuster or now a really nifty trailer!

iLife

iWeb

iWeb is a great way to start learning how to create awesome websites. With its ease of use and powerful tools – you can create a spectacular website in no time. As with the other "i" applications – iWeb starts out with a Welcome screen that allows you to access a getting started video or video tutorials. Use my guide to get your feet wet and Explore! Explore! Explore!

If you click on close on the Welcome screen – iWeb will bring up the screen shown below. There are two windows inside of this window. The one to the left shows you what theme

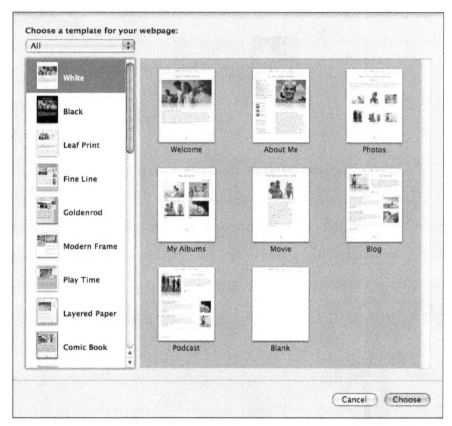

you want to use. On the right, you can chose what format you want to use – Welcome, About Me, Photos, etc. Note – after you start a site – iWeb always brings up that site when launched again. You have to select a New site to start over.

iWeb – Main Screen

Below is a sample of the main work environment of iWeb. Notice that I chose a Photos template and that shows up under **Site** all the way on the upper left corner. Photos currently are the one and only webpage in my site. The white area (can be different if you chose a different theme) is the preview of the webpage. The icons with a black background behind them make up the Media section of the program. I will go over the other elements on the pages to follow.

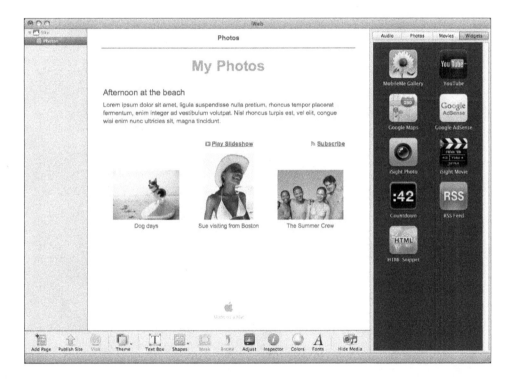

 This button adds another page to your site. It brings up the theme and template chooser shown on the previous page.

 By default, this button sends your site to **MobileMe** and publishes it (makes it visible to the outside world). You can setup **MobileMe** to use another domain (added cost to you). This maybe wise or necessary – depending on your needs. Below is the dialog box that comes up when your site is done being published. Notice that is gives you the actual web address (http://web.me.com/gdurdik/site) and that you can announce it the world in an email by clicking on Announce.

Your site has been published.

Your site is located at:

http://web.me.com/gdurdik/Site

You can announce your website with an email message containing your website address, or view the website in your browser.

(Announce) (Visit Site Now) (OK)

 This button just brings up the current "live" site on the web.

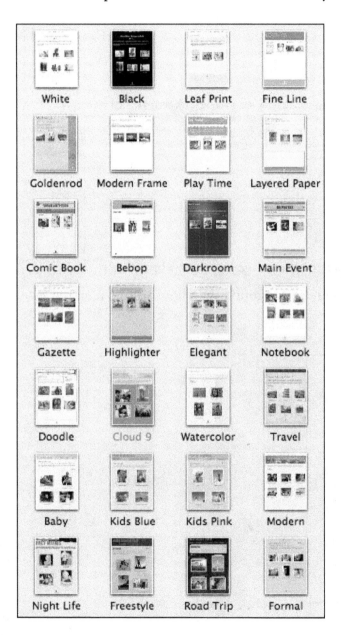 This button allows you to bring up the themes and change the one you have. Below is a sample of all of the themes available to you.

This button allows you to create a free-floating text box.

 This button allows inserting a variety of shapes. A sample of a few of them is shown to right.

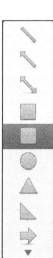

This button allows hiding or masking part of the image in your webpage. An example of this is shown below. The lighter area around the photo will be removed when the mask is applied.

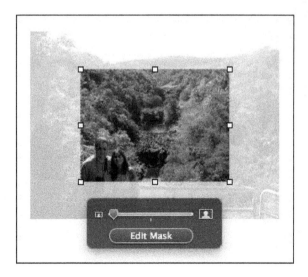

This does what it says – it rotates your graphic 90 degrees at a time.

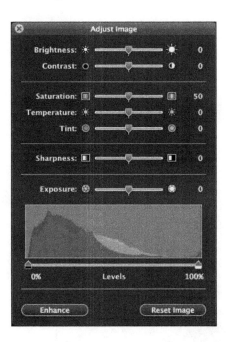

The **adjust button** allows you to modify your image in a variety of ways. On the bottom left is the Enhance button. The application attempts – the best it can – to make the image look its best.

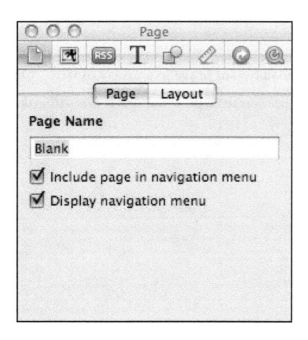 This button brings up the **Inspector dialog box.** This is shown below. Notice that there is a row of eight icons. Each one represents a different function. The Palm tree icon is the Photos inspector and the T is Text inspector.

 This button brings up the color palettes you can choose. Each one is unique. A sample of one of the palettes is shown to the right.

This button deals exclusively with text. The window it brings up is shown to the right.

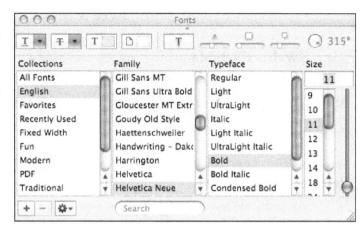

This button hides or shows the Media section of program. Media includes audio, movies, photos or widgets.

iWeb Menus

iWeb - iWeb Menu

This menu contains two important items. The first is **About iWeb**. This tells you what version you are running. The second is **Preferences....** This is discussed below.

iWeb - iWeb Menu - Preferences

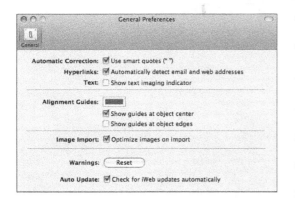

This menu consists of four groups of options. The first group – at the top of the screen has three options. They are **Automatic correction** – decide if you want to use smart quotes, have iWeb **automatically detect email and web addresses** and last – **show the text imaging indicator**. The second group deals with **Alignment guides**. You can set their color and decide if you want them for the object center and/or object edge. The next option deals with Image imports. By default, it will optimize images on import. This is recommended. The last group asks if you want to reset warnings and updates. You can have iWeb automatically check for updates.

iWeb – File Menu

New Page	⌘N
New Site	⇧⌘N
Close	⌘W
Save	⌘S
Revert to Saved...	
Publish Site Changes	
Publish Entire Site	
Visit Published Site	
Check for New Comments	
Submit Podcast to iTunes...	
Set Up Google AdSense...	
Set Up Personal Domain on MobileMe	
Page Setup...	⇧⌘P
Print...	⌘P

In this menu you can create a new Page or Site, save your work, publish new site changes or the entire site. You also visit the published site here as well. You can setup **Google Adsense...** and a personal Domain on **MobileMe**. Last, you can print your work as well.

iWeb – Edit Menu

Undo Unmask	⌘Z
Redo	⇧⌘Z
Cut	⌘X
Copy	⌘C
Paste	⌘V
Paste and Match Style	⌥⇧⌘V
Delete	
Delete Page	
Duplicate	⌘D
Select All	⌘A
Deselect All	⇧⌘A
Find	▶
Spelling	▶
Special Characters...	⌥⌘T

Here you can **undo** the last action you preformed or **redo** it if you decide to keep the change. You can **Cut** items out of you work, **Copy** items found in your work and **Paste** copied items into your site. Paste and Match Style will paste what is copied – exactly. You **Delete** an object or **Delete a whole page**. You **Duplicate** an item here as well. Use **Select all** if you want to make perhaps a change to the font on the whole page. You have access to a search tool via the **Find** command and a spell check via **Spelling**. Last, you have access to **Special Characters**. That is – symbols or graphics found in a font that you would not normally see.

iWeb – Insert Menu

Simply, this menu gives you the option to insert a variety of items into you document. This includes Hyperlinks, text boxes, shapes, a button or a widget. Choose... gives you access to an item not listed above.

iWeb – Format Menu

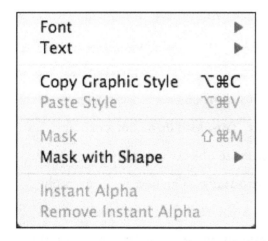

This menu allows you to modify Font and Text characteristics. You can copy a Graphic Style, Mask a picture or Mask with a shape. Last, you have the option to use Instant Alpha – which attempts to make the color you chose in a picture transparent.

iWeb – Arrange Menu

Bring Forward	⌥⇧⌘F
Bring to Front	⇧⌘F
Send Backward	⌥⇧⌘B
Send to Back	⇧⌘B
Align Objects	▶
Distribute Objects	▶
Rotate Clockwise	⌥⌘R
Rotate Counter Clockwise	⌘R
Flip Horizontally	
Flip Vertically	

This menu is broken down into four sections. In the first section we have **Bring Forward, Bring to Front, Send Backward or Send to Back.** Think of your document as having many layers to it. Each graphic or item has its own layer. Let's say there is a text box with a short sentence in it. You want to put a picture behind it. Make sure that the picture is over the text and select either Send Backward or Send to Back. After this is done, your text is on visible on the screen and the picture is the background for it. The next section allows you to **align objects – Left, Center, or right, Top, Middle or bottom.** You can **distribute objects vertically or horizontally**. The next section simply allows you to decide how you want to **rotate an image**. The last option on this menu allows you to **Flip an image Horizontally or Vertically**.

iWeb – View Menu

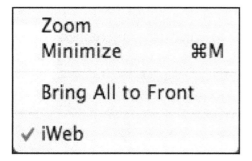

Show Layout	⇧⌘L
Hide Inspector	⌥⌘I
Show Colors	⇧⌘C
Show Adjust Image	
Hide Media	

Show Layout – shows the invisible guides in you webpage. **Inspector** – show or hide – is a tool to modify many characteristics of you website. You can also have iWeb show the **Colors palette**, or **Adjust image tool**. Last, you can have iWeb hide the Media section of your main window. In the example I used earlier – the Media section is showing.

iWeb – Window Menu

Zoom	
Minimize	⌘M
Bring All to Front	
✓ iWeb	

Zoom – Makes the window as large as it can on your screen. **Minimize** – shrinks you work and places an icon of it in your Dock. Click on this icon to bring your work back on the screen. **Bring All to Front** – If you have many applications open at once – this option will bring all open windows associated with iWeb and bring them in front of all other windows.

iWeb – Help Menu

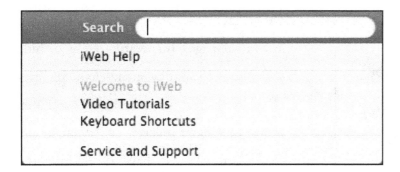

I am not a webmaster. I hopefully provided enough info to get your feet wet and start creating a site. If you have further questions or want to watch more in-depth video tutorials – use this menu.

So.... Got something you want to world to see or hear about? Photos, Resume or Product? iWeb is a great application to get started creating simple to complex web pages. Start small – Think Big when it comes to creating your website.

iLife

GarageBand

Want to be the next rock star? GarageBand is an awesome tool to create your own music. It even now offers lessons to help you learn certain instruments. As with the other applications I touched upon – I will go over the working environment and the GarageBand menus. So, let's get started with the default startup screen. As you will notice from

the screen shown above – you have access to Getting Started Videos or video tutorials. Click on close when you want to get the party started.

The next screen – shown below – is the access point to a variety of ways to use GarageBand. If you just want to start composing – click on **New Project** and choose what instrument or type of project. (Songwriting or Podcast). I will go over in great detail (I am not musician so I will keep things as simple as I can) the main environment of a new project. But first... I will go over the other cool and exciting things you can do with GarageBand.

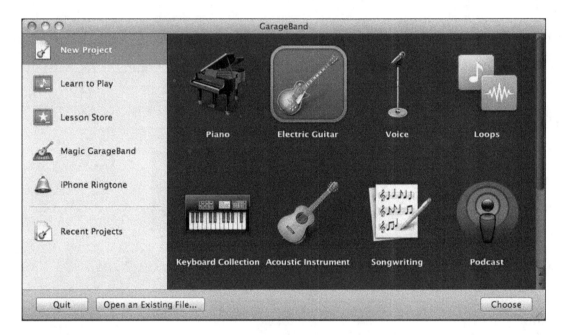

Learn to Play

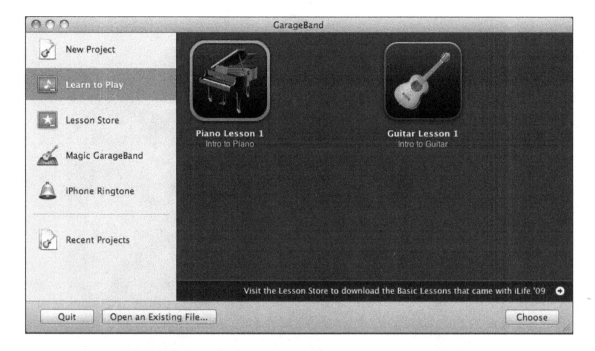

Here GarageBand gives you access to a sample piano or guitar lesson.

Lesson Store

Here you can purchase additional lessons for GarageBand. It includes Basic lessons and Artist lessons (shown on the previous page).

Magic GarageBand

Prefer jammin' with a band? Magic GarageBand creates a band atmosphere for all of the types of music shown in the screen above.

I chose FUNK. Notice that the Piano has a spotlight on it and it states it my instrument. This means when you are jammin' – you will be the pianist.

Notice the **My Instrument** section on the bottom left of the screen. Do you see the

little tuning fork? If you click on it – it turns blue. This will then give you

access to the keys shown in the example above. Note – you can have GarageBand

play a snippet or the Entire Song.

 The big red button starts recording your piece.

This is the PLAY button.

Open in GarageBand After you done jammin' you can have the piece brought into the main editing window and further edit your work.

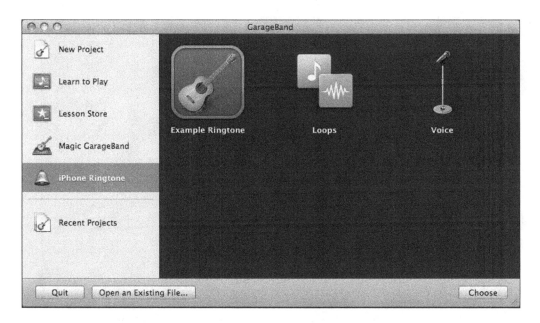

iPhone Ringtone – Create your own ringtones and send them to iTunes. The choices to begin the process are shown above.

Back to creating a new masterpiece via New Project.

The first screen you will see is the one to the right. Notice that you have to give it a name and designate where it is to be saved. In the section below you decide what the tempo is going to be, set a Signature and Key.

GarageBand Main Window

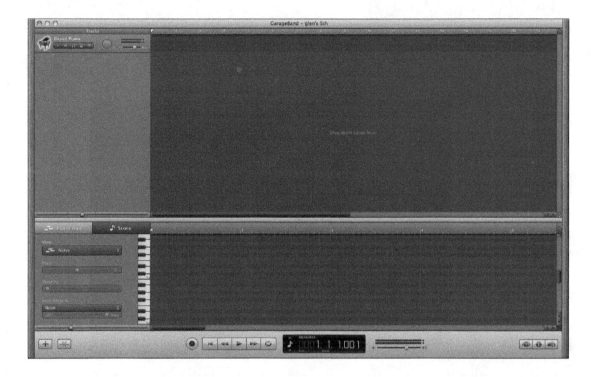

There are two main sections. The first is the **Track list** – (Grand Piano name and icon in the example above.

The section below is where you compose the notes – **Track editor**. Note the piano keys – this is what you use to create your songs. Below is an example of a window with notes already entered into the composition. Beethoven I am not.

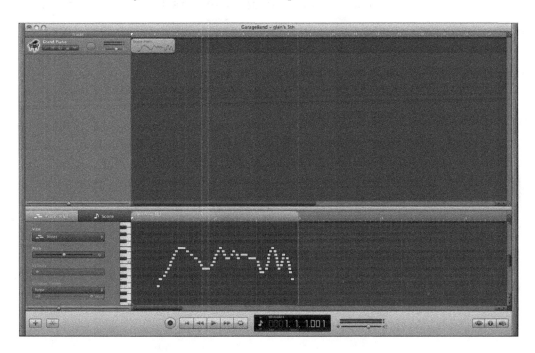

I just want to elaborate on the track controls a bit. Notice that the image above has a green tint to it. This means that the instrument is selected and the options for it can be adjusted.

The Red Circle – enables or disables recording on the selected track.

The Speaker Icon – mutes or "unmutes" the track.

The Headphones Icon – solos or "unsolos" the track. (All other instruments are turned off)

The Lock Icon – locks or unlocks a track. It also renders it to your hard drive, which frees up processing power.

Down Arrow Icon – shows or hides automation for a track.

Space Bar – Pauses playback or recording.

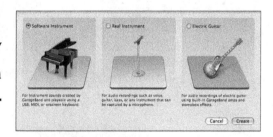

This button creates a **New Track**. You are given the choice of a **software instrument, real instrument or electric guitar**. This is shown to the right.

IF you chose a **Software Instrument** – the following window is displayed on the right side of your working environment. Chose the instrument you want and just click on it. It will then appear as "Shimmering Flute" inside your Track list for example.

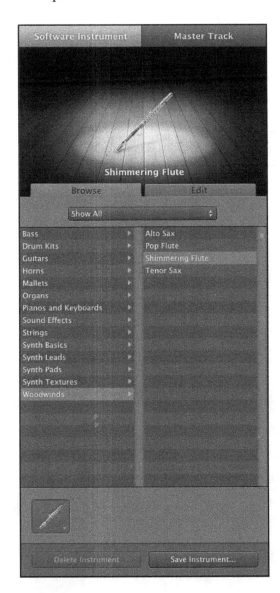

 This button shows or hides the Track editor.

This button is the record button.

 These buttons deal with maneuvering around inside your track. Arrow pointing to the left with a line next to it – brings you back to the beginning of your work. The DOUBLE Arrows advances your track forward or backward. The big triangle in the middle is the PLAY button. The arrows in a circular motion – turns cycling on or off. If it is on – GarageBand will cycle only the music already composed. It will get to the end of the section and then go back to the beginning and start over.

 This "LCD" screen shows you the measures (and other items via the Control Menu) found in you work.

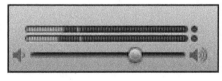 This shows you the left and right volumes and gives you to change the volume with the slider on the bottom.

 This button brings up the Loop Browser. The choices are shown below.

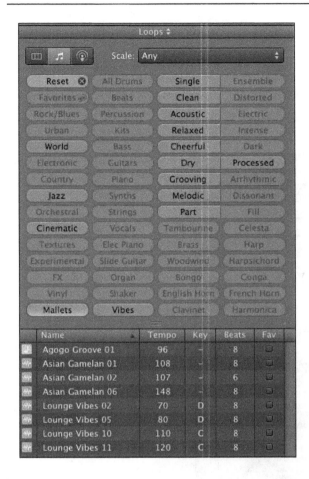

Name	Tempo	Key	Beats	Fav
Agogo Groove 01	96	–	8	☐
Asian Gamelan 01	108	–	8	☐
Asian Gamelan 02	107	–	6	☐
Asian Gamelan 06	148	–	8	☐
Lounge Vibes 02	70	D	8	☐
Lounge Vibes 05	80	D	8	☐
Lounge Vibes 10	110	C	8	☐
Lounge Vibes 11	120	C	8	☐

This button displays track info. It hides or shows other options or features of GarageBand that is displayed on the right hand side of the main window.

 This button brings on the **Media Browser**. This is shown to the right. Notice that you have access to **Audio, Photos and Movies**. There is a search feature located at the bottom of the screen.

GarageBand Menus

GarageBand – GarageBand Menu

About GarageBand	
Preferences...	⌘,
Shop for GarageBand Products	
Provide GarageBand Feedback	
Register GarageBand	
Check for Updates...	
Learn about Jam Packs	
Services	▶
Hide GarageBand	⌘H
Hide Others	⌥⌘H
Show All	
Quit GarageBand	⌘Q

This menu contains a few important items. **About GarageBand** states what version you are running. **Preferences...** are discussed below. **Shop for GarageBand Products** brings you to an Apple store website dealing with items for this product. You can look elsewhere for similar items not found there. **Check for Updates** – goes online and checks to see if there are any updates. **Learn about Jam Packs** – you can purchase more loops and more instruments via the website it brings up.

GarageBand – GarageBand Menu Preferences - General

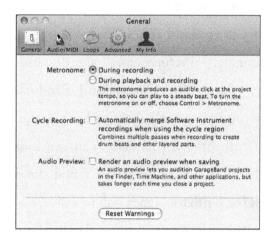

Metronome can be set to be on only during recording or recording and playback mode. **Cycle Recording** – can be set to automatically merge software instruments inside the cycle region. **Audio Preview** – creates an audio preview that can be used in the Finder, Time Machine and other apps.

GarageBand – GarageBand Menu Preferences – Audio/MIDI

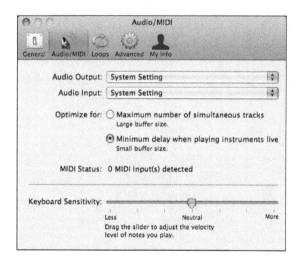

Audio Output can be set for System Setting or Built-in Output. **Audio Input** can be set for System Setting, Built-in Microphone or Built-in Input. You can have GarageBand be optimized for a large number of simultaneous tracks (large buffer size) or have a minimum delay when playing instruments live (small buffer size).

If you have a MIDI device attached it would show up next to MIDI Status.

Last, you can set keyboard sensitivity. The default is neutral.

GarageBand – GarageBand Menu Preferences – Audio/MIDI

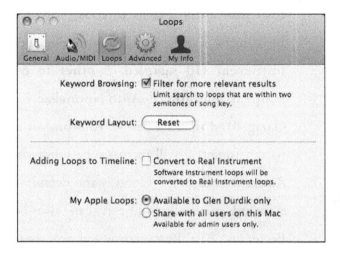

You can have **Keyword Browsing** filter for more relevant results (loops that are within two semitones of song key). You reset the **Keyword Layout** if you wish. You are given the option her to convert added loops to Real Instruments. Last, you can make you Apple loops only available to you or share with other (admin) users on your Mac.

GarageBand – GarageBand Menu
Preferences – Advanced

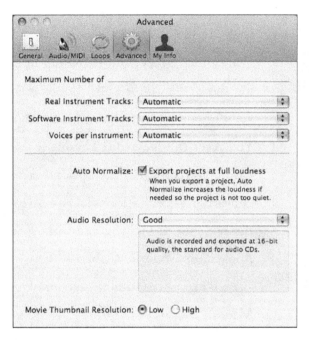

Here you can set the maximum number of Real Instrument Tracks **(8-255)**, Software Instrument Tracks **(8-64)** and Voices per Instrument **(10 sampled, 5 other to 64 sampled, max other)**. **Auto Normalize** – if GarageBand thinks a part of your project is to soft (quiet) it will increase the loudness. **Audio Resolution** – Good is the default – standard for audio CDs. It can also be Better and Best. Best records and exports at 24-Bits.

GarageBand – GarageBand Menu Preferences – My Info

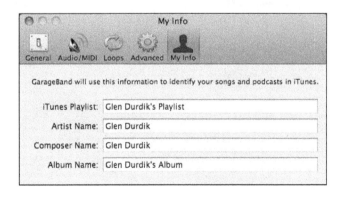

This option will determine what Playlist is to be used and who the composer of the projects is.

GarageBand – File Menu

New	⌘N
Open...	⌘O
Open Recent	▶
Close	⌘W
Save	⌘S
Save As...	⇧⌘S
Revert to Saved	
Page Setup...	⇧⌘P
Print...	⌘P

Here you can create a project, open a saved work, open recent work, close the work or save or perform a **Save As...** If you perform a **Save As...,** you can also Archive the Project (this saves Real Instrument Apple loops into the project so that the project can be safely moved to another Mac) or use Compact Project (this saves a 128kbps AAC format to reduce the size of the file).

GarageBand – Edit Menu

Undo Recording	⌘Z
Redo	⇧⌘Z
Cut	⌘X
Copy	⌘C
Paste	⌘V
Delete	
Delete and Move	^ ⌫
Select All	⌘A
Add Marker	P
Split	⌘T
Join	⌘J
Add To Loop Library...	
Special Characters...	⌥⌘T

In this menu – you can **undo** the last action taken or **redo** it if you decide to keep the change. **Cut** – removes item you have highlighted. **Copy** – takes what you highlighted and puts it in the System "clipboard" for future use. **Paste** – Put what you just copied in the work at the place you have chosen. **Delete** – removes the item you highlighted. **Delete and Move** – deletes and allows you to move the item elsewhere. **Select All** – highlights all tracks and all the notes housed in them.

Add Marker adds a notation in the Audio Region. **Split** allows you to start playing for a location different from the beginning of your project. **Add to Loop Library**... you can add a section of your work to the standard set of Loops . **Special Characters** - Adds access to special symbols not normally seen when use fonts.

GarageBand – Track Menu

Hide Track Info	⌘I
Show Arrange Track	⇧⌘A
Show Master Track	⌘B
Show Podcast Track	⇧⌘B
Show Movie Track	⌥⌘B
New Track...	⌥⌘N
Delete Track	⌘⌫
Duplicate Track	⌘D
New Basic Track	⇧⌘N
Fade Out	

This menu allows you to chose what Tracks you want to show. This includes Arrange, Master, Podcast and Movie. You can add, delete or Duplicate a track here as well. **Fade Out** – allows you to have the track volume slowly decrease to silence.

GarageBand – Control Menu

✓ Metronome	⌘U
Count In	⇧⌘U
✓ Snap to Grid	⌘G
Show Alignment Guides	⇧⌘G
Ducking	⇧⌘R
Show Loop Browser	⌘L
Show Media Browser	⌘R
Hide Editor	⌘E
Show Chord in LCD	⌘F
Show Time in LCD	⇧⌘F
✓ Show Measures in LCD	⌥⌘F
Show Tempo in LCD	^⌘F
Lock Automation Curves to Regions	⌥⌘A

This menu deals with several different items. You can have the Metronome and Count IN showing. **Ducking** is used to lower track volumes so that voices can be heard better. Good for Podcasts. You can show or hide various elements. This includes the Loop and Media Browser; the LCD is the blue digital readout in your main window. You can have Chords, Time, Measures and Tempo shown in this LCD display if you wish. **Lock automation Curves to Regions** - each track has automation curves for various settings. Here you can specify and lock in these curves,

GarageBand – Share Menu

Send Song to iTunes
Send Ringtone to iTunes
Send Podcast to iWeb
Send Movie to iDVD

Export Song to Disk...

Burn Song to CD

Ready to share your work with the rest of your fans? Here you can send a song or ringtone to iTunes. You can send a Podcast to iWeb to be part of a website. You can burn a song to a CD. You can export your song as an MP3 or AAC format.

GarageBand – Window Menu

Minimize	⌘M
Zoom	
Keyboard	⌘K
Musical Typing	⇧⌘K
✓ glen's 5th.band	

Minimize – takes the current window and removes from your monitor and places it into your Dock. To get it back on the screen – click on the icon in the Dock. **Zoom** – makes the window the largest it can be on your screen.

Keyboard – Shimmering Flute

To the left – is the keyboard when you chose Keyboard in this Window Menu

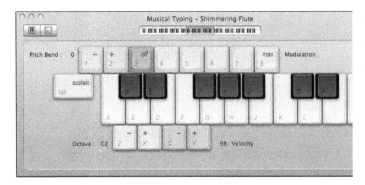

To the left is the interface when you chose Musical Typing in the Window Menu.

GarageBand – Help Menu

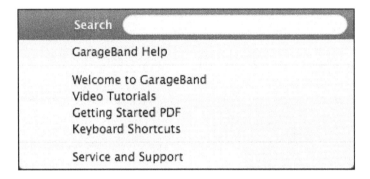

Got a question not answered in this short guide – go to this menu for the answer. You can type in a topic question, view Video Tutorials, a Welcome Video or view a Getting Started PDF.

What's New in GarageBand '11?

There are a few spectacular new items in this version. I will go over them in the next few pages.

Learn to Play: This feature was in the older version, but it has been updated. The first screen you encounter is below.

Note: Chord trainer is a new option. Guitar Lessons, Piano Lessons and Artist Lessons are now on the top of the window. Also, notice that you can download the basic lessons via the Internet for this program.

Lesson Store – Start Screen. Click on Guitar Lessons, Piano Lessons or Artist lessons.

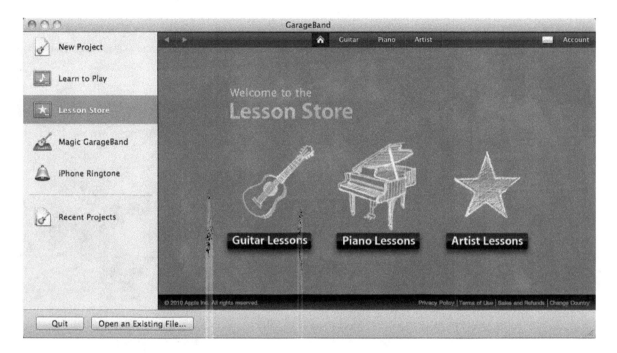

Below is the window you will see if you choose **Lesson Store – Guitar.** You can chose between **Basic Guitar**, **Rock Guitar** or **Blues Guitar**.

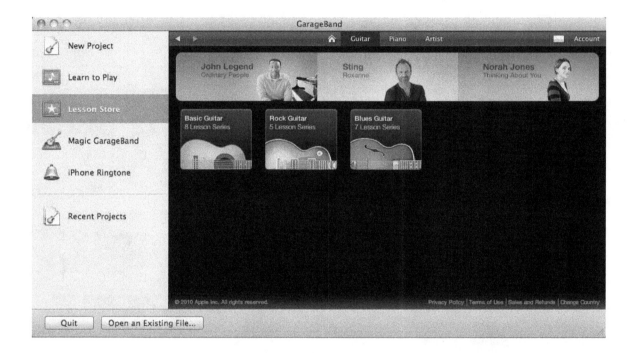

Below is the window if you chose **Basic Guitar**. It shows all the lessons available and gives you the option to download all at once or lesson by lesson.

Below is the window if you choose **Piano**. You can chose from **Basic, Pop or Classic** Piano lessons.

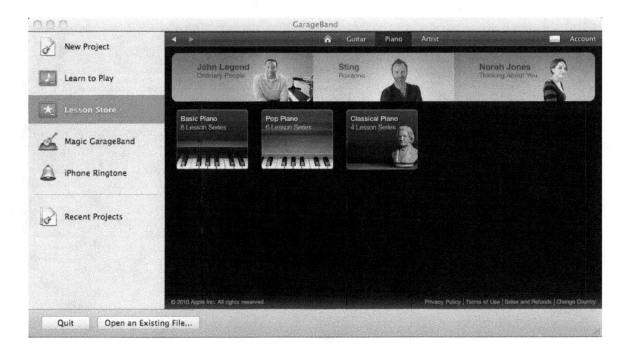

Below is a screenshot of an actual lesson-taking place. It is hard to see – but on the bottom you can see a timeline of items to be covered, what speed you want the lesson to be played (half – normal), a Play/Pause Button, Replay and a Volume Slider.

Flex Time.

This new feature allows you to easily change the timing of your recording. You can move, shorten or stretch notes. You just click and drag the waveform in your editor window to edit a note or beat. Your changes are highlighted so you know what you changed. Just click on the Flex Time Button to compare the original with the revised version.

Groove Matching.

Your masterpiece seems to suffer from a lack of rhythm? Grove Matching is here to the rescue. Just select one of your tracks and make it the Groove Track. GarageBand then makes all other tracks sync with this "master" Groove track. You do not have to have all the tracks sync if you want. This also allows Apple Loops to have better integration with your project.

Guitar Amps and Stompbox Effects.

This new version of GarageBand adds seven more guitar amps. (total of 12)

This new version of GarageBand adds five new stompbox effects. (total of 15)

So…when will I hear your new song on the radio?? I hope that I got you feet wet in using GarageBand. I am not a musician – so this program is still a mystery in some aspects. I do think it is a great tool to start learning how to write music for the beginner and a good tool for the more experienced to lay down some mean tunes.

iLife

iTunes

iTunes started a revolution – music downloads started to soar after Apple introduced iTunes and the iTunes Store. iTunes is also available for Windows users as well. You just got your new Mac and want to create an audio library of all your CDs. You might want to purchase a song you just heard on the radio. iTunes provides the solution to both of these situations. I will go over all the elements of iTunes in the next few pages. However, when you first launch iTunes – there are a few questions that have to be answered before you can begin importing or purchasing. The first screen that arises is the welcome screen. This is shown below.

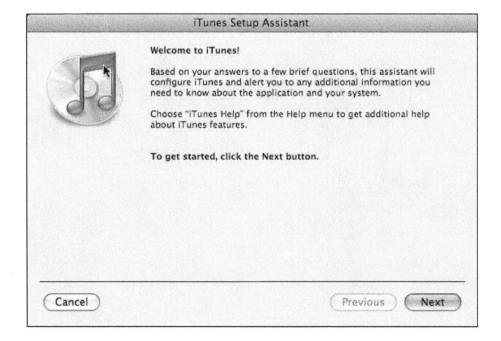

Click next to move on. The next screen – shown below asks if you want to use iTunes for Internet audio content. This should be set to Yes for most users. There are other Internet audio applications that must be downloaded and installed to see or hear the content in some websites.

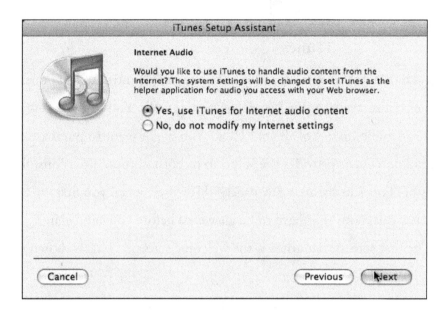

The next screen shown below asks if you want iTunes to import content that you already have stored on your hard drive. Notice that it only searches your Home Folder – you may have content elsewhere that you may want to add later.

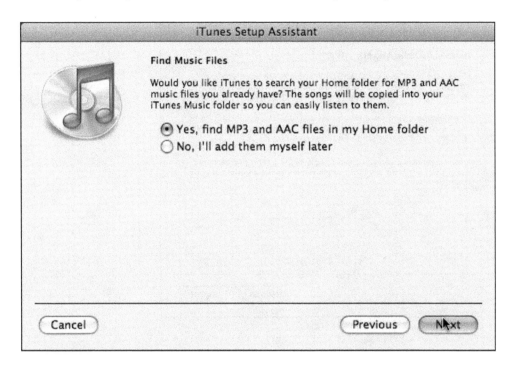

The next screen – shown to the left asks if you want to keep your music folder organized. Most users will keep this on an say Yes. It makes it easier to find you content in searches if the info was changed automatically.

The last screen that arises deals with album artwork. Basically, if you want an albums' artwork to be part of your library – you have to create and iTunes store account. It is free – but requires a credit card account to start.

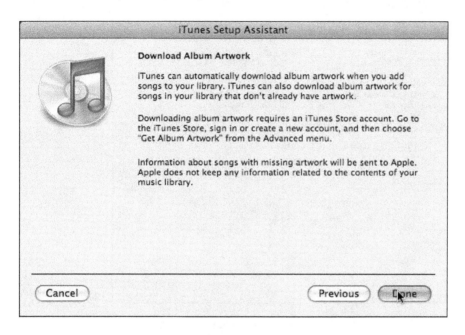

iTunes – Main Windows

Music

Above is the window you will see if you click on MUSIC under LIBRARY on the top left side of the iTunes main window. Note the two items under DEVICES – Glen Durdik's iPod and Wonderful World. If you have an iPod (which I will describe in detail later) this is where it would show up. Wonderful World is a CD and it too would show up under Devices.

Movies

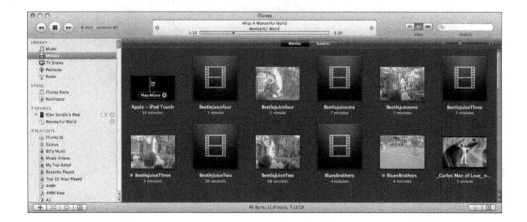

Above is the window you will see if you click on MOVIES under LIBRARY on the top left side of your iTunes main window.

TV Shows

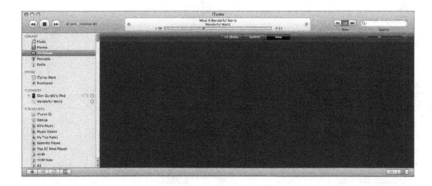

Above is the screen you will see if you click on TV SHOWS under LIBRARY. It is broken down into three categories – TV Shows, Genres and New.

Podcasts

Above is the screen you will see if you click on PODCASTS under Library. Note that is broken down into three categories – Podcasts, Categories and New. Note also that you have access to a Podcast Directory at the lower right of the screen and that you can unsubscribe to Podcasts here as well.

Radio

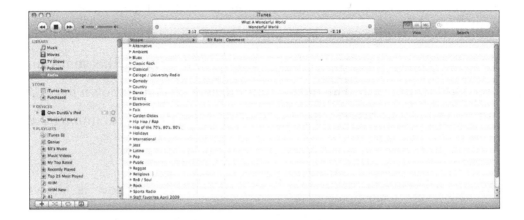

Above is the screen you will see if you click on RADIO under LIBRARY. This gives you access to list of streaming radio streams in one convenient location. Under each heading (Blues, Classic Rock) is a list of stations, their bit rate (higher number better = better audio quality, but more data to download causing it to be slower or pause) and a description of the station.

Store

The next category after LIBRARY is iTunes STORE. This is where you can download music, TV Shows and Movies. In the example on the last page, I searched for the group "GENESIS." Notice that is brought items in various categories such as ARTISTS, ALBUMS and MUSIC VIDEOS. Below that lists all the songs and other items in a basic straight list. The next item - Purchased is not shown here. All items purchased via iTunes go into this folder. You can then drag them into a new playlist or one that already exists.

Note: When you download an item – the Downloads window is shown below Purchased. The spinning arrows mean it is downloading. The number next to it displays how many items you are currently downloading. This is show on the next page.

DEVICES

If you insert a CD or attach an iPod – this is where these items will show up. I will go over iPod (touch) features later on. You can import a CD by clicking on the IMPORT CD icon on the bottom right of the screen.

PLAYLISTS – iTunes DJ

Above is the first screen you will see if you first click on iTunes DJ. If you click on continue, the playlist iTunes has started off with is shown. An example of this is shown below.

To change the default settings, click on Settings... on the bottom right of your DJ window.

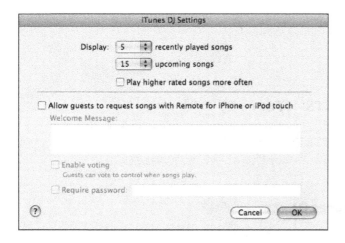

This screen is divided into two sections. The first determines what you want displayed in the iTunes window. This includes recently played songs and upcoming songs. If you decided to rate your songs - you can also have higher rated ones played more often. The second deals with accessing iTunes via an iPhone or iPod Touch. You can turn this feature on or off, enable voting and give a password to access to the DJ list.

Playlist – Genius

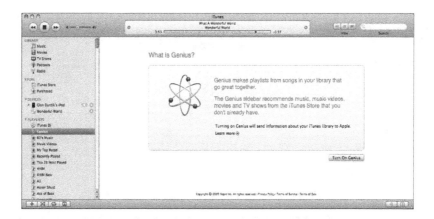

Want to find music from artists you never heard of that fits your music tastes? Enter Genius. Once setup – iTunes will suggest songs available in the store that you might like based on your library. Above is the first screen you will see when setting Genius up.

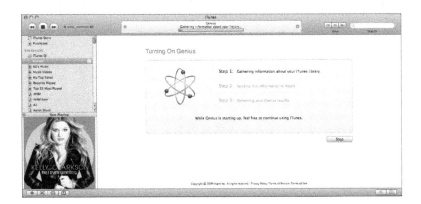

The next steps are shown above – Gather info, send to Apple, and get results.

After it is setup, just click on a song (In Your Eyes) in the example above and click on

the Genius Button on the bottom right of the screen [icon] to show what iTunes thinks what you might like in your Library.

The button next to Genius Button is the Genius Sidebar Button. This brings up music found in the iTunes store (for purchase) that you might like to also. This is shown below.

Playlist – User Created

All other playlists are shown in the examples above are created by myself. I chose to create playlists based on an artist's name.

Views Available to view Media

List View

This view is the most comprehensive option.   Notice that it gives the Name, Time, Artist, Album by Artist, Genre and Rating (and more not shown above). This is what is on by default. You can add Release Date, or sample rate for example.

Grid View

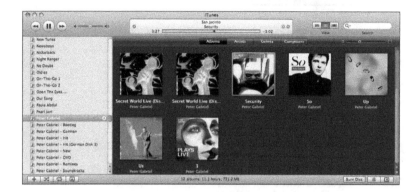

This option is not as descriptive as the List View. Albums are displayed by their cover art. If you click on the album you like, you are given a similar List View – but with a small picture of the cover art of the album on the left.

Cover Flow View

This is the most visual of the three views. Notice there is a slider below the album cover shown up. You navigate the playlist by dragging this slider back and forth. The contents of the highlighted album are shown below in a list view.

Main Window – Icons not previous mentioned

 Red (far right) closes the window. Yellow (middle) shrinks the window into the Dock. Click on the icon in the Dock to bring it back to full size. Green (far right) - Makes the window as large as possible or displays just the basics – a "MiniPlayer" shown below.

 When clicked, it brings you first to the beginning of the track playing. If you continue to click it – it will go backwards down the playlist.

 Plays the track you have currently selected. If music is playing – the Play button turns into a Pause button.

This button skips to the next song in the playlist.

 This slider determines the volume in iTunes. You might have to adjust the system volume to get the volume you want. (System maybe set too low or too high)

This window shows the time elapsed, Title of the Song, Artist, Album and time remaining of the song currently playing. You also have access to the Genius feature here.

 Mentioned in previous section.

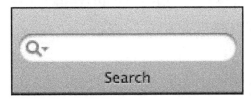 Here you can search for an item in your Library. Note – you have to have the category under LIBRARY to search the entire Library. Otherwise, you are just searching within the current playlist.

 This button creates a new Playlist.

 This button turns a Shuffle feature ON or OFF.

This button is the Repeat button. By default it is turned off. If you click on it once, you get a blue symbol, which means it will repeat the entire Playlist. If you click on it a second time, you get a blue symbol with a Number 1 inside of it. This will repeat only the currently playing song. If you click it a third time – you turn off the repeat feature.

This button hides or shows Album Covers in the Playlist section of the iTunes main window.

9118 items, 27.4 days, 43.51 GB This section on the bottom – in the middle – displays the total items in a playlist, the number of hours (and days) it would take to listen to the entire playlist and the actual hard drive space the playlist takes.

Burn Disc If you want to make a copy of your songs or playlists – choose the item and click on Burn Disc. The following window will appear...

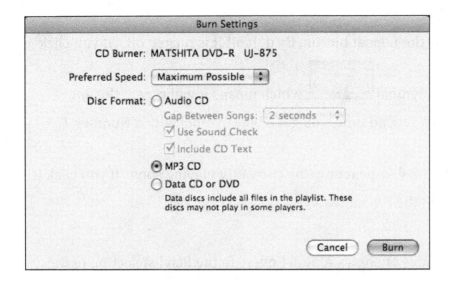

Notice that you can burn Audio CDs (works with all CD players), MP3 CDs – some CD players and computers or a Data CD or DVD. An MP3 CD can store a whole lot more music that a regular CD, but may not work in older CD players. A Data disc will 99% of the time only work on a computer.

iTunes – Menus

iTunes – iTunes Menu

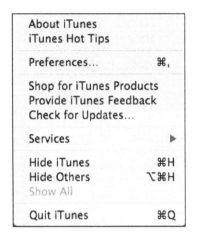

There are a few important items in this menu. **About iTunes –** tells you want version you are running. **Preferences...** are discussed next. Check for Updates goes online and checks for any updates for the software.

iTunes – iTunes Menu – Preferences - General

Here you give your Library a name. This is important if you share your Library over a network. **Show:** Decides what is displayed on the left-hand side of the iTunes Window. **Note:** If you have and iPod Touch or iPhone – you should have Applications set to SHOW. Insert CD settings and Import Settings are discussed on the next page. You should have iTunes automatically retrieve CD track names and check for software updates.

The options to the left are the options you have when you insert a CD into your computer. Show CD is the default choice.

Import Settings – There are tow items to consider here. The first is what Encoder you want to use. I chose MP3 as my choice as I like to make custom MP3s CDs from my Library. Some of the other Encoders offer higher quality sound however.

These are the choices for Encoder. Each has its strengths and weaknesses. For ease of use of burning CDs I chose MP3.

The Next step is the Setting for the Encoder. The example to the left is for MP3 encoding. The higher the kbps the better the sound quality.

iTunes – iTunes Menu – Preferences - Playback

The first three settings (**Cross fade, Sound Enhancer and Sound Check**) modify the way the music is played.   I have never used the Sound Enhancer – so try it and see if you like it. Sound Check is nice in that it keeps the volume at certain level. Play Movies and TV Shows and Play Music Videos can be either the   iTunes   window   or

in artwork viewer
✓ in the iTunes window
in a separate window
full screen
full screen (with visuals)

You can set the Audio Language, have Subtitles turner on, play videos in standard definition and last – show close captioning when available.

iTunes – iTunes Menu – Preferences - Sharing

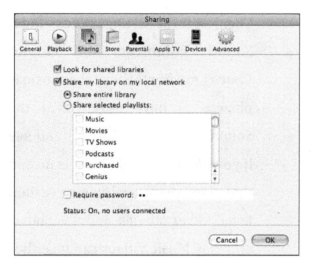

If you are a network – you can search for shared libraries or share your own. Note that you can share just selected playlists and that you can assign it a password.

iTunes – iTunes Menu – Preferences - Store

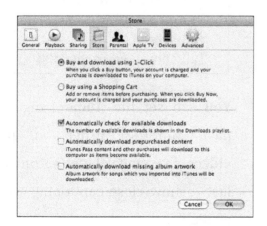

The top part of this window deals with the way you purchase your media from the store. Buy and download using 1-Click will purchase you item(s) by just confirming your purchase. The second – places the items in a traditional Shopping Cart and is only purchased when you click on Buy Now. In the lower half, you can have iTunes automatically check for downloads, automatically download prepurchased content and last – check for and download missing album artwork.

iTunes – iTunes Menu – Preferences – Parental

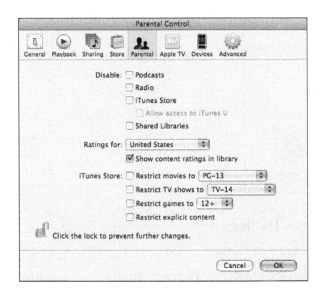

Want to block your little ones for harsh media? Use this preference to modify what they can see or download. The first section disables – if you want – Podcasts, Radio, iTunes Store or Shared Libraries. The second section sets what are the age limits for movies, TV shows and games. You can also set a broader category by restricting explicit content. **Note: DO NOT** forget to lock this preference after you are done setting it up. Hey – kids are smart these days.

iTunes – iTunes Menu – Preferences – Apple TV

If you own an Apple TV – this is where you would set it up to link with your iTunes.

iTunes – iTunes Menu – Preferences – Devices

iTunes makes a backup of your devices before it performs updates. Note that I have one device and one backup in the list. You can disable iTunes from automatically syncing iPhones and iPods here as well. You can have the program look for remote speakers connected via AirTunes, disable iTunes control over remote speakers and allow iTunes to take control over remote speakers. Last, you can disable iTunes from looking for iPhone or iPod Touch Remotes.

iTunes – iTunes Menu – Preferences – Advanced

The first section of this window deals with the Music Folder. Note that there is a default location, but it CAN be changed to another one if you prefer. Next, I would leave the default choice of keeping the iTunes Music folder organized and to automatically copy files to the iTunes Music folder when adding an item to the library. Next, you have three options to ponder. The streaming buffer size determines the size of the file be streamed. iTunes probably is your best bet for Internet playback for most of your needs, so leave it Set to use iTunes. Reset all dialog warnings – clears all warnings. When you minimize iTunes – you get a MiniPlayer. If you click on the "Keep MiniPlayer on top..." This player will always be the top (visible) window on your monitor. The same reasoning applies for the movie window option. The **Visualizer** is a cool feature that syncs music to an ever-changing visual image. By default it is only shown in the iTunes window. Here you can make it the full screen. Grouping of compilations when browsing is the last option here.

iTunes – File Menu

New Playlist	⌘N
New Playlist from Selection	⇧⌘N
New Playlist Folder	
New Smart Playlist...	⌥⌘N
Edit Smart Playlist	
Close Window	⌘W
Add to Library...	⌘O
Library	▶
Get Info	⌘I
Rating	▶
Show in Finder	⌘R
Show Duplicates	
Sync iPod	
Transfer Purchases from iPod	
Page Setup...	
Print...	⌘P

Here you can create a **New Playlist** (no contents), a **Playlist from a selection** of songs or create a **Smart Playlist**. A **Smart Playlist** will take items from you library based on your criteria. **Get Info** – gives you details on the item you highlighted. You can also rate your selection here as well. Show in Finder brings up the window of the actual location of your song. You can Sync your iPod here if it is not done automatically and transfer purchases made away from your Mac on your iPod.

Back Up to Disc...
Consolidate Library...
Export Library...
Burn Playlist to Disc
Import Playlist...
Export Playlist...

These are the options found in the Library Submenu. Note that you can backup your entire library to a disc or export it as well. Also you can burn a Playlist to disc here.

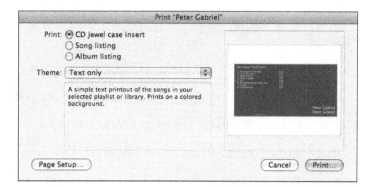

This is the screen that comes up when you select Print. You print a CD Jewel case insert – shown on the left, Song listings or Album Listing. The themes that can be printed are shown below.

✓ Text only
Mosaic
White mosaic
Single cover
Text only (Black & White)
Mosaic (Black & White)
Single side (Black & White)
Large playlist (Black & White)

iTunes – Edit Menu

This Edit Menu is similar to other Edit menus. You can **undo** or **redo** an action, have access to **Cut** and **Delete**, **Copy** and **Paste** functions. You can also use **Select All** to highlight all items shown in the main window (usually a playlist). **Special Characters** allows having access to characters found in fonts that are not normally seen.

iTunes – View Menu

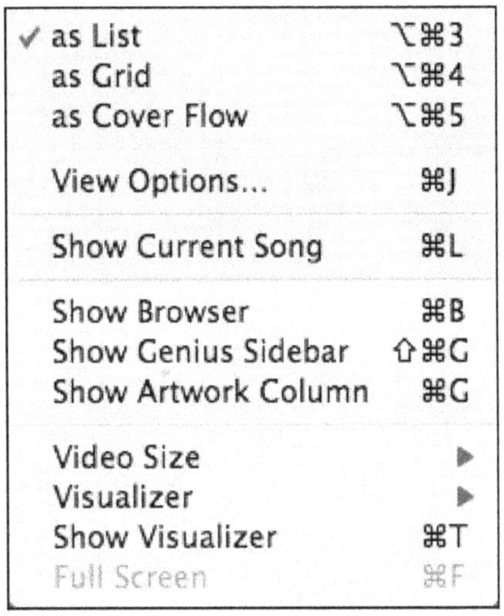

✓ as List	⌥⌘3
as Grid	⌥⌘4
as Cover Flow	⌥⌘5
View Options...	⌘J
Show Current Song	⌘L
Show Browser	⌘B
Show Genius Sidebar	⇧⌘G
Show Artwork Column	⌘G
Video Size	▶
Visualizer	▶
Show Visualizer	⌘T
Full Screen	⌘F

The first three options are List, Grid or Cover Flow. I showed what these are earlier in this guide. View Options are shown below the Edit Menu. If you are jumping around iTunes while listening to a song – the playlist window will reflect where you are looking. If you select **Show Current Song** – it returns the window back to the playlist the song is located. An example of Show Browser and Genius Sidebar are shown below and on the next page. Show Artwork column just adds the album cover to the current Playlist.

View Options.

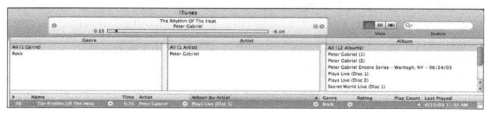

This is what the playlist window looks like if you have the Browser showing. It has Genre, Artist and Albums on top of the playlist currently in use.

This is what the Genius Sidebar looks like.

Video Size can be any of the sizes shown on the left.

The Visualizer is a cool feature that syncs various shapes and colors with the song you are playing. iTunes has more than one choice and you can download others. An example is shown to the left. Note – by default it only plays in the iTunes window. You can have it play Full Screen by choosing the last item in this menu.

iTunes – Controls Menu

Stop	space
Next	⌘ ⋯→
Previous	⌘ ←⋯
Next Chapter	⇧⌘ ⋯→
Previous Chapter	⇧⌘ ←⋯
Audio & Subtitles	▶
Shuffle	▶
Repeat	▶
Eject Disc	⌘E

Turn On Shuffle
✓ By Songs
By Albums
By Groupings

The first item here is very useful to remember. To stop a song or video – hit the SPACE BAR. Next and Previous – go forward one track or back one track. Next or Previous Chapter deals with Audiobooks. Audio and Subtitles with videos. Eject Disc just removes the CD from your computer.

Shuffle Submenu - can be also done for songs by clicking on the [⤫] button.

Repeat Submenu – can also be done by clicking once for All and twice for one on the  button.

iTunes – Store Menu

Back	⌘[
Forward	⌘]
Home	⇧⌘H
Search...	
Turn Off Genius	
Update Genius	
Create an iMix...	
Create Ringtone...	
Authorize Computer...	
Deauthorize Computer...	
Sign Out	
View My Account (phoenix737@nyc.rr.com)...	
Check for Available Downloads...	

This first part of this menu deals with Navigating through the iTunes store. Next it deals with the Genius feature of iTunes as this involves the store for suggestions to buy. An **iMix** allows you to share a Playlist with the rest of the world. You can only create a Ringtone for your phone from songs purchased from the iTunes store. **Authorize or Deauthorize Computer** – you can only have up to five computers under one iTunes account. For most people this is not a problem – but **REMEMBER to DEAUTHORIZE your computer before you erase**

the hard drive or give it to someone else. iTunes stores hidden data and erased that account will be permanently ON that Mac or PC. You can sign in, sign out and check your iTunes account here as well. Check for available downloads – if you have items not yet downloaded to your computer – this option will find them and resume the download.

iTunes – Advanced Menu

Open Audio Stream...   ⌘U
Subscribe to Podcast...

Create iPod or iPhone Version
Create Apple TV Version
Create MP3 Version

Get Album Artwork
Get CD Track Names
Submit CD Track Names
Join CD Tracks

Deauthorize Audible Account...

If you know the website (url) of streaming audio – this is where you can access it. You can subscribe to Podcasts in this menu. The next section of the menu deals with converting media to work with Apple's portable devices (iPhone or iPod) or an Apple TV. If you want to create large MP3 CD from songs not in the MP3 format – this menu allows you to convert them here. Note that you will have the original and the MP3 version in your library. If you want to delete one or the other – I suggest that you add KIND to the view options and do a Search for the item and delete the one you no longer need. **Get Album Artwork** and **Get CD Track Names** go out via iTunes to search for the items you are missing. Some items may NOT be found. You can add (Submit) CD track names here if you wish. Join CD tracks takes out the spaces between songs normally put in when importing. Last, you can deauthorize and Audible Account here.

iTunes – Window Menu

Minimize	⌘M
Zoom	^⌘Z
✓ iTunes	⌥⌘1
Equalizer	⌥⌘2
Bring All to Front	

Minimize – shrinks the current window and places it in the Dock. To get it back – click on the icon in the Dock. **Zoom** – either shrinks the iTunes window to the MiniPlayer view or brings it back to its normal Player Window. If you have a lot of applications open – you can select **Bring All to Front** to bring all iTunes windows to be in front of all others.

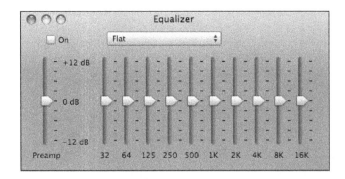

To the left is the **Equalizer** function of iTunes. There are a number of presets (Flat shown) and can be turned on or off.

iTunes – Help Menu

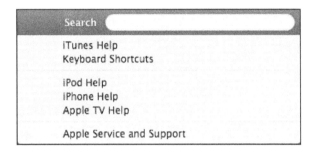

The concept of iTunes is simple. As you have seen – there are a lot of details to know about in order to fully take control of iTunes and use it effectively. I hope I covered the basics in this manual. However, if you have other questions – go to this menu for further insight or tips.

....and now to iPod use......

Using an iPod (touch) with your PC and iTunes

OK. Just got a new iPod and don't know what to do next. I have an iPod Touch so I will go over the items associated with it and iTunes. Before I begin – let me state that iTunes backs up your iPod whenever an update is made to it. The screens involved are shown on the next page.

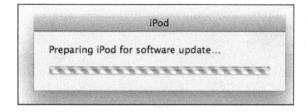

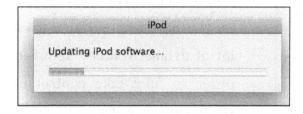

Now back to beginning – sort of. If something is wrong with your iPod or you want to just erase it and start over from scratch – there is a Restore Feature that brings you iPod back to its original settings. In order to write a more complete manual – this is what I did to my iPod. The Restore window is shown below. Note that your brand new iPod would NOT have a backup to restore from.

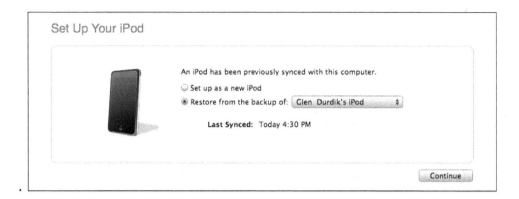

If you select Setup as a new iPod – the screen below comes up after you click on

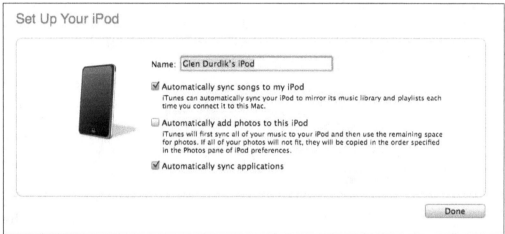

Continue. Here you can name your iPod, set iTunes to automatically sync songs to your iPod (can be turned off later), automatically add photos to the iPod (as many as it could fit) and last – automatically sync applications. Applications only work on iPod Touches and iPhones.

After this done – your iPod now shows up under DEVICES in your iTunes window. The plug inside the battery icon means it is attached and charging. The arrow pointing

upwards is what you need to click when you want to remove your iPod from your Mac. Never disconnect it without doing this. It could corrupt your iPod. Bad.

If your iPod is clicked on in the main window – the following screen will appear on the right on the main window. The window is broken down into four categories. On the top are the tabs of what type of media is on your iPod. Below that is the iPod section, which tells you the name, the capacity, the software version and serial number of your ultra-cool iPod Touch. The next section is Version. Here you will find out if your iPod needs and update or check for an update. I mentioned earlier there is a button to Restore your iPod to its original settings. If you see the example

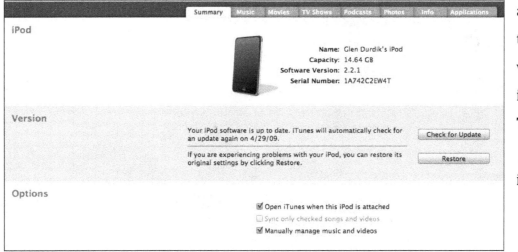

above – this is where it is found. The last section is the Options section.

You have three options to configure. Do you want iTunes to open when the iPod is attached? Do you only want to sync checked songs and videos? And last – Do you want to manually manage music and videos?

Before I continue with the other tabs – let just mention that below this window is a visual bar that describes what is on the iPod and how much space is left. This is shown below.
Empty...

With media on it...

One last thing – kind of important I guess. To the right of the capacity graph is the

Sync button. [Sync] iTunes does not make any changes to the iPod until you click on this button.

Music Tab

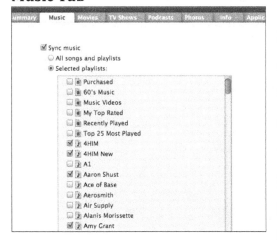

Note that you have three options here. One – do you want to Sync you music? You might want to use your iPod for videos or applications only. The next two options are – Do you want to sync ALL songs and playlists? Or Selected playlists? Many people probably have a lot more music that would fit on an iPod Touch – so selected playlists is the best option. In the example to the left – notice this is what I have selected. ALL of the items with a check mark next to them will be synced when I chose to sync my iPod.

Movies Tab

First note the cutoff message on top - you can transfer rented Movies from the iTunes store to your iPod. This is similar to Music. Items with a check mark are synced, you can use Selected Movies or Selected Playlists, you can choose all movies or just unwatched ones.

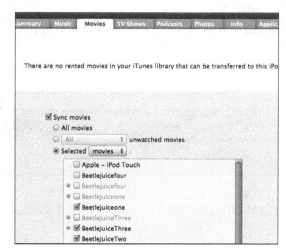

TV Shows Tab

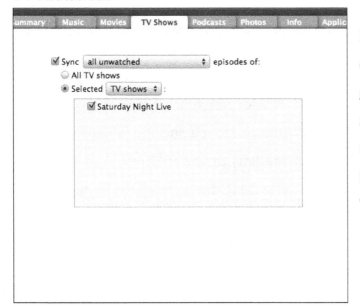

Here you can again sync all items or selected ones. You are also given the choice to NOT sync TV shows by unchecking the box next to sync. TV Shows has an interesting submenu for SYNC. This is shown below.

Podcasts Tab

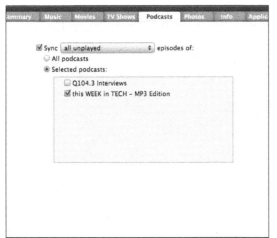

This is similar to the other tabs – Sync ALL Or Selected. As with TV Shows, there is a custom SYNC Submenu. This is shown to the right. If you uncheck the box next to Sync – it will not sync the items.

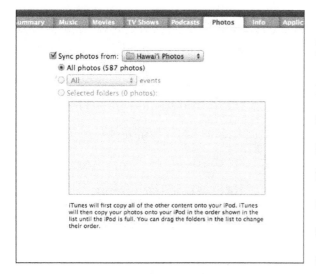

Photos Tab

First – you are given the opportunity to sync or not sync photos. You can SYNC photos from a specific folder (shown on the left) or from iPhoto. You again can choose if you want all the items or just a selection. Note that iTunes has to optimize your photos to work on your iPod. This process is shown below.

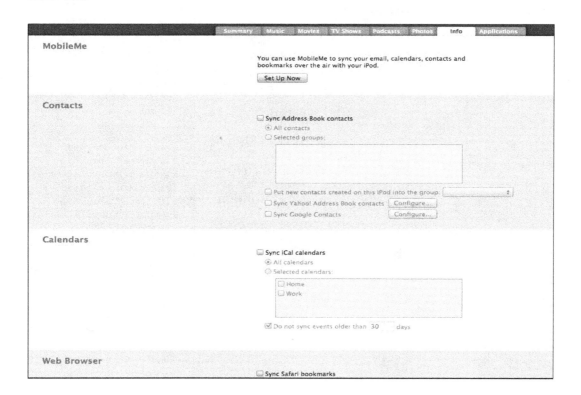

Info Tab

This tab has a lot of options to deal with. The first option is to setup **MobileMe** access. I discussed **MobileMe** in my guide to OS X.5. You have the ability to manually sync Address Book contacts, iCal calendars and Safari bookmarks.

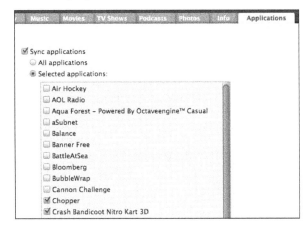

Applications Tab

Nothing new here. Choose if you want all applications or selected ones. You also given the choice to sync or don't sync applications at the very top.

So you have selected all the items you need synced and you click on the SYNC button. The following screen will appear.

Updating Files on "Glen Durdik's iPod"
Copying 816 of 1474: Last Goodbye

It is copying over 1,474 items and it is up to item number 816 in the example above.

New Features of iTunes 9

iTunes is now up to version 9.0. Most of what was covered in the previous pages of this manual. I will now go over the key differences of this new version.

New Splash Screen on Launch: There are a few new items when you iTunes first comes on your screen. This is shown below. You now have easy access to videos on variety of topics. I still prefer a paper manual that I can read at my leisure.

Home Sharing: With this new feature – you can copy purchased items to any Mac on your network. The first step is to start Home Sharing on ALL of the Macs you want connected with the SAME iTunes Store account. To activate it, go to the Advanced Menu and select Turn on Home Sharing. The screen on the next page is what pops up when you select this option.

Type in your password and click on the **Create Home Share** button on the bottom right of your screen.

If you look at playlists on the left side of your screen – you will now see icons of available libraries.   There are two types of libraries. In the example above – the brown house with a musical note on it means I can copy from or to this library. Open to everything. The other icon – not shown – is blue "pages" and has a note in it. These libraries can only be read – not copied. The icon to the far right of the library (arrow pointing up) ejects this library and it is no longer connected to your library.

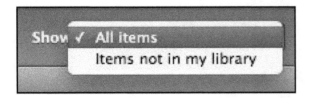

If you access a shared Home Share – there are two options of note on the bottom of the screen. The first – shown above is the **Show** button. This is on the bottom left of your screen. As you can see, if you click on it, you are given two choices. View all items or Items not in my library.

The second is **Settings**. This is found at the bottom right of your screen. Here you can set preferences as to what you want automatically transferred to your library from the library you are currently accessing. This is shown below.

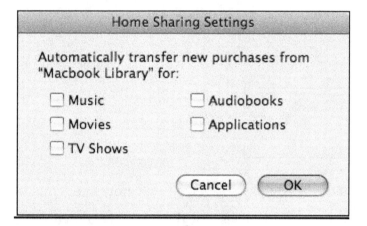

Genius Mixes – iTunes 9 builds upon the addition of the Genius function in iTunes 8. With mixes, you are given a grid with selections all based on Genius data. The Genius mix icon is shown below.

A sample Genius mix is shown below.

iTunes Store – new Interface - The iTunes store is completely different than before. Basically, explore the new items and see what you can find as usual. This is shown below.

There are a few new things that I want to highlight. One, you can now have the store go full screen. To do this, go to the iTunes menu, select Preferences, Store option. One of the choices is view store as full screen. This is show on the next page.

If you want to back to the normal view, there is a Home icon on top of the store window. Click on this icon and iTunes returns to the normal view.

On the screen, if you see an album you want more info on or purchase songs/album. Move your mouse over the album's icon and you will notice a small "i" appear on the bottom right of the icon. Click on "i" to get further info and the ability to purchase the item or songs. This is shown above.

iTunes LP/ Extras - This is an exciting new way to view music purchases. This feature is brand new and there are just a few artists that have them available for download. Think of it as purchasing a "multimedia experience" – not just a album. Special features might be unreleased videos, interviews, unreleased photos, etc.

New iPod transfer windows – iTunes has changed the way you sync data to your iPod. I selected a few to show you – so you can compare to the older version.

Music

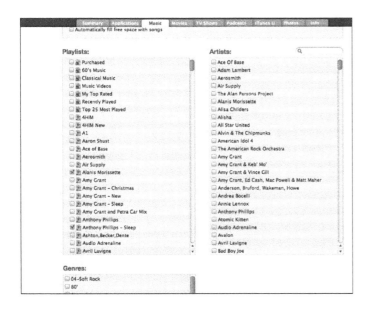

Movies

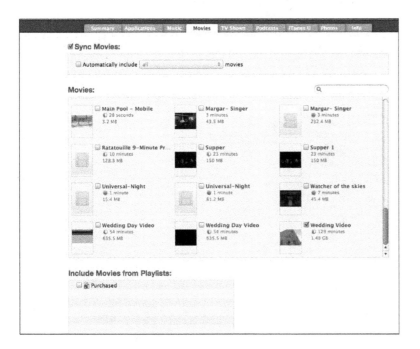

Applications

Photos

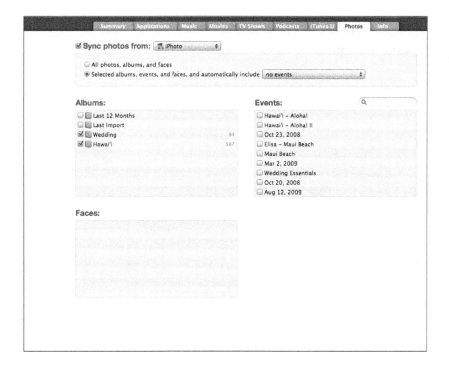

Where did the Mini-Player go?

I admit I could not figure out how to activate this feature until I did some research. Background – the Mini-player shrinks the current window to a small, minimal info window. This is show below. You normally would click the green button to shrink it or enlarge it. Not anymore. **NOTE: Update your iTunes to the latest version and the regular Mini-Player button is activated again.**

In this version of iTunes, you can either hold down the OPTION key while clicking on the green button or going to the **View** Menu and select **Switch to Mini-Player**.

What's New in iTunes 10?

(new icon for iTunes)

There are few minor changes in this new version and one major new addition. I will discuss this new addition first – Ping. This is a new social network setup by Apple for iTunes users connect to other users, their favorite musicians and help find new artists as well.

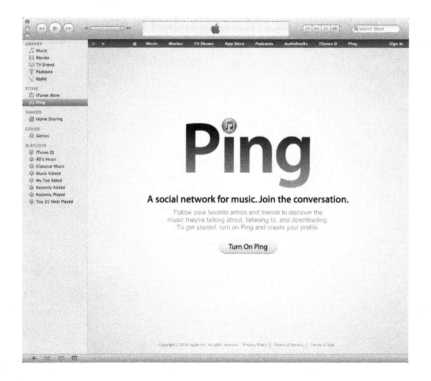

Above is the screen to turn on Ping. You have to setup a separate profile for Ping.

Ping is located in the left-hand sidebar – under the **STORE** heading. This is shown below.

I have already added artists to my Ping Network. This is shown below.

It is really easy to add new friends or musicians. On the home page, type in a name of someone you are looking for. This is shown below.

As you can see below, I typed in Michael W. Smith and got the results shown. You just click on the **Follow** button and all updates for the artist will now show up on you Ping homepage.

Below is the confirmation.

If you have Ping activated, a Ping submenu is shown when you click on a song in your Library. This is shown below.

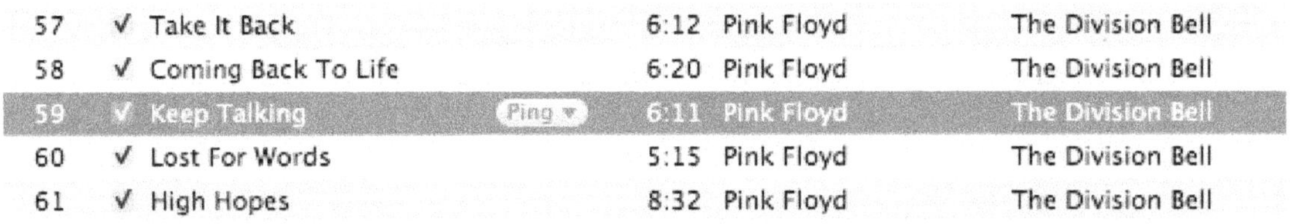

57	✓ Take It Back		6:12	Pink Floyd	The Division Bell
58	✓ Coming Back To Life		6:20	Pink Floyd	The Division Bell
59	✓ Keep Talking	Ping ▼	6:11	Pink Floyd	The Division Bell
60	✓ Lost For Words		5:15	Pink Floyd	The Division Bell
61	✓ High Hopes		8:32	Pink Floyd	The Division Bell

If you click on Ping, you get the following choices...

57	✓ Take It Back	6:12	Pink Floyd
58	✓ Coming Back To Life	6:20	Pink Floyd
59	✓ Keep Talking		
60	✓ Lost For Words		
61	✓ High Hopes		
62	✓ The Post War Dream		
63	✓ Your Possible Pasts		
64	✓ One Of The Few		
65	✓ The Hero's Return		
66	✓ The Gunner's Dream		
67	✓ Paranoid Eyes		
68	✓ Get Your Filthy Hand Off My		
69	✓ The Fletcher Memorial Home	4:12	Pink Floyd
70	✓ Southampton Dock	2:12	Pink Floyd

Ping
Like
Post...
Show Artist Profile

Show in iTunes Store
Keep Talking
Pink Floyd
The Division Bell
Rock

You can **Like** a song, **Post** something on you Ping Homepage or **Show the Artist's profile**. The other section that comes up gives you options to view in the iTunes Store.

The controls for closing the iTunes window, minimize do the Dock and start the Mini-Player now have a new orientation. This is shown above.

iPod Connections: There a few changes to the way iTunes interacts with your awesome iPod. One change is that the capacity bar tells you how much space you have left in real time.

Below are examples of other changes.

Apps Screen – Now shows how it will appear on your iPod Touch or iPhone. You can organize how the apps appear on you iOS (iPad, iTouch, iPhone) device as well.

Music Screen – Notice that it now includes "**Include Music Videos**," "**Voice Memos**," and "**Automatically fill free space with songs**."

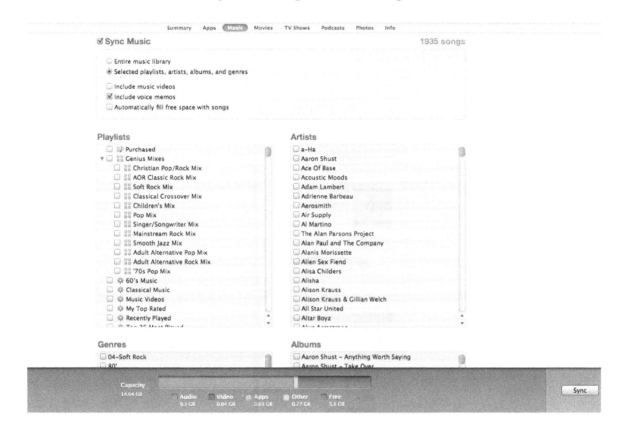

The other choices (Movies, TV shows, Photos, etc.) basically remained unchanged.

www.ingramcontent.com/pod-product-compliance
Lightning Source LLC
Chambersburg PA
CBHW080149060326
40689CB00018B/3907